With Sails to the Wind

By V. Gilbert Beers

Illustrated by Helen Endres

MOODY PRESS • CHICAGO

What You Will Find in This Book

© 1977 by V. Gilbert Beers
Library of Congress Catalog Number:
ISBN: 0-8024-9570-2

Printed in the United States of America

SAILING TO ADVENTURE

	Page
Sailing with a Runaway, *Jonah 1–2*	6
Runaway Mini, *A Muffin Family Story*	9
Sailing Through a Storm, *Mark 4: 1, 35-41*	12
The Hundred Pound Cream Puff, *A Muffin Family Story*	14
Sailing with Fishermen Friends, *John 21: 1-14*	18
Indian War Parties and Fire-Breathing Dragons, *A Muffin Family Story*	22
Sailing for Jesus, *Acts 13: 1-6*	26
With Sails to the Wind, *A Muffin Family Story*	29

CHILDREN OF PROMISE

Angel in the Fire, *Judges 13*	34
The Strongest Men in the World, *A Muffin Family Story*	37
The Woman Who Kept Her Promise, *1 Samuel 1: 1-20*	40
Too Many Promises, *A Muffin Family Story*	43
The Miracle Child, *Luke 1: 5-25, 57-66*	46
A Walk Through the Woods, *A Muffin Family Story*	48

A SLAVE WHO RULED THE LAND

The Jealous Brothers, *Genesis 37*	54
Tuff and Taffy, *A Muffin Family Story*	57
Slave in a Strange Land, *Genesis 39*	60
The Tea Party Under the Tree House Party, *A Muffin Family Story*	63
A Strange Day in Joseph's Life, *Genesis 40: 1–41: 46*	66
A Time for Yes or No, *A Muffin Family Story*	69
A Time to Forgive, *Genesis 42: 1–45: 16*	72
A Ruff Day, *A Muffin Family Story*	76

WHO IS THAT CHILD?

A Night That Changed the World, *Luke 2: 1-20*	82
The New Pony for Tony Maloney, *A Muffin Family Story*	87
Rich Gifts for a New King, *Matthew 2: 1-12*	90
The Castle and the Pigpen, *A Muffin Family Story*	93

The Journey to Egypt, *Matthew 2: 13-23; Luke 2: 39*	98
Take Care of Your Family, *A Muffin Family Story*	102
A Visit to God's House, *Luke 2: 41-50*	106
The "What If" Game, *A Muffin Family Story*	110

MARCHING THROUGH STRANGE PLACES

Food from Heaven, *Exodus 15: 1, 22–16: 36*	116
Eggs, *A Muffin Family Story*	120
With God on a Mountain, *Exodus 19–20*	124
Rules, *A Muffin Family Story*	127
The Golden Calf, *Exodus 32*	130
King of the Ice Cream Castle, *A Muffin Family Story*	133
A House for God in the Wilderness, *Exodus 35–40*	138
The Tablernacle Jar, *A Muffin Family Story*	141

MINI'S WORD LIST   144

TO PARENTS AND TEACHERS

Each of us remembers some special place where stories became real-life adventures, a crossroads where fantasy spoke of reality. It was here, at this special place, that many of life's important lessons were learned.

Three books in The Muffin Family Picture Bible series speak of such a place. The first in the series, *Through Golden Windows*, shows the meeting place of Bible and everyday life at the golden windows. A tagalong tree is that kind of place in *Under the Tagalong Tree*. Now, in this volume, Maxi and Mini sail off to adventures beneath the cloudy presence of ships such as those on which Paul sailed.

Since the Bible stories are a creative retelling of the Scriptures, you may wish to use the Bible itself wherever possible as you share the adventures in this volume with your children.

SAILING TO ADVENTURE

Sailing with a Runaway

JONAH 1—2

Jonah was frightened. He had just heard God call his name. "What does He want?" Jonah wondered.

Then God called again. "Go to Nineveh," He told Jonah. "Tell the people about their sin. Tell them how I will forgive them if they ask Me."

"No!" Jonah whispered. "Not Nineveh! Those wicked people don't want to hear about God. They will kill me if I go there."

Jonah wondered what he could do. He certainly did not want to go to Nineveh. But where could he go?

"I will run away," Jonah thought. "I will go far away where I can hide from God."

Jonah ran away to Joppa, where he found a ship that was ready to sail. Before long, he was on his way to Tarshish, as far away as he could go from Nineveh. Tired and afraid, he lay down and fell asleep.

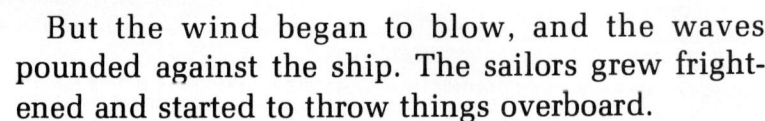

But the wind began to blow, and the waves pounded against the ship. The sailors grew frightened and started to throw things overboard.

It wasn't long before the captain of the ship found Jonah asleep. "Get up!" he shouted. "Pray that your God will help us!"

Jonah felt strange as he asked God for help. He was running away from God, but the captain wanted him to ask God to be with him.

As the storm grew worse, the sailors tried to find if someone had done something wrong. They were superstitious and believed in gods that would punish them for doing wrong things. Perhaps that had caused the storm. At last they found that it was Jonah.

"What have you done?" the sailors asked.

"I'm a runaway," Jonah answered. "I'm running away from God."

"How can we stop the storm?" they asked.

"Throw me into the sea," said Jonah.

The sailors didn't want to do that, but the storm was getting worse.

When the sailors threw Jonah into the sea, a great fish came up and swallowed him. Then the storm stopped, and the wind and waves became quiet.

For three days and three nights, Jonah lived inside the great fish. It was dark and lonely, and Jonah hurt because of the strong juices inside the fish.

Jonah didn't want to run away from God now. He prayed and prayed for God to be with him and help him. Then God made the fish put Jonah out on the shore.

For a while, Jonah was probably too weak and tired to go anywhere. But when he could, he went straight to Nineveh.

Jonah was no longer a runaway. He knew now that he could never find a place to hide from God—not on a ship, in a fish, or even in a strange city filled with evil people.

WHAT DO YOU THINK?

What this story teaches: God expects His people to obey Him and not run away.

1. When God asked Jonah to work for Him, what did Jonah try to do instead? Why couldn't he run away from God?
2. When God asks you to do something which you may not want to do, should you try to hide? What should you do? Would you want God to try to hide from you when you ask Him to do something important?

Runaway Mini

"Mini!" Mommi called from the kitchen. "Will you please set the table for me?"

Mini barely looked up from the book she was reading. "Ummmph," she mumbled.

"Be sure to put on the placemats first," Mommi added. "And while you're at it, would you please set the salt and peppers on?"

"Ummmph," came another sound from behind the book.

"Oh, one other thing," Mommi called. "Will you please feed Ruff and Tuff before dinner?"

Mini looked up from her book. "Why doesn't Maxi do some of that?" she asked, almost to herself. "All I do is work." Of course Mini knew that Maxi would say the same thing if Mommi had asked him to do it.

Mini had barely finished saying that when Mommi called again. "Oh, Mini, one other thing," she said. "Be sure to fill the water dish for Ruff when you feed him."

Before Mommi could call again, Mini threw down her book and stomped out to do her chores. She did not look very happy as she set the table, filled Ruff's water dish, and fed him. Then she brought out a can of cat food and gave Tuff her dinner.

"You won't mind helping me wash the dishes tonight, will you?" Mommi chimed from the kitchen. "Then we can change the sheets on your bed before you do your practicing on the piano."

Mini didn't want to stay inside to hear about more work, so she stomped out of the front door. "Don't go far," Mommi called. "We'll have dinner in about forty-five minutes."

"I won't be here!" Mini grumbled softly. "I'll . . . I'll run away! That's what I'll do! Then I won't have to work so hard any more."

Mini wasn't sure where she would go or what she would do, but the first thing was to start somewhere. So she headed downtown.

But before she had reached the first little shops, Mini noticed that the sky was getting darker and darker.

"Oh, oh!" she whispered. "Looks like a big storm. What will I do now?"

Running away wouldn't be much fun in a storm. Especially since she had no umbrella or raincoat.

When Mini came to the stop light at Main Street, the wind began to blow, picking up dust and chewing gum wrappers and blowing them into Mini's face. Bright flashes of lightning crackled across the sky, followed by loud rumbles of thunder.

Mini was afraid now. This was going to be a bad storm, and Mommi and Poppi didn't even know she was gone.

While Mini waited for the light to change, the rain began to fall in big drops. Mini decided she would make a dash for the toy shop across the street. She looked this way and that. There were no cars coming, so she ran across the street.

But the policeman on the corner blew his whistle and yelled at Mini. "Are you trying to get killed?" he shouted.

Just then the rain began to fall in torrents. By the time Mini reached the toy shop she was soaked.

"Downtown alone today?" the toy shop man asked Mini. Mini nodded. She was soaked to the skin and water dripped from her clothes to the floor.

"Soon as I put this package in the back, I'll call your folks for you," the man said. "You can give me your number, and they can pick you up."

Mini gulped. What would she say to them? No, she didn't want that! As soon as the man went to the back, Mini ran out into the rain and ducked into the entry of another shop down the street.

But when Mini looked up in the window, she saw a big poster of a shark. His mouth was open and it looked like he was ready to swallow her.

Mini let out a little "yik" and ran out into the rain again. This time she kept on running until she

10

reached home. Mommi was busy in the kitchen and didn't hear Mini come in.

It took only a few minutes for Mini to get into dry clothes and hang her wet ones over the rack in the corner. She quickly dried her hair with Mommi's hair dryer and was the first one to sit down at the dinner table.

"Well, well," said Poppi. "Isn't it nice that none of us has to be out in the rain this evening?"

Mini gulped.

"After dinner we'll read the story of Jonah from our new Muffin Family book, *With Sails to the Wind*," said Poppi. "It's about a man who tried to run away from God and got into trouble in a storm."

Mini gulped again. She just could not imagine why anyone would want to run away! Especially with a storm coming.

"Mommi," said Mini. "May I help you wash the dishes tonight? Then we can change the sheets on my bed before I practice the piano."

Mommi smiled. Mini smiled too. It would be fun to help do some of the chores tonight.

LET'S TALK ABOUT THIS

What this story teaches: We are happier when we obey God, and those He puts over us, than when we try to run away from what they expect.

1. How was Mini like Jonah? What was Jonah running away from? What was Mini running away from?
2. What changed Mini's mind about doing chores?
3. Do you ever get angry because you have to do chores? What did you learn from this story about doing cheerfully what you are asked to do?

Sailing Through a Storm

MARK 4:1, 35-41

All day the people had crowded around Jesus. They had pushed. They had shoved. Everyone wanted to be close to Jesus so that he could be healed or helped.

At last Jesus was tired. It was time to leave the crowd and go to some quiet place alone with His disciples.

"We will go to the other side of the sea," Jesus told His disciples.

Jesus went with His friends into a boat. While the friends raised the sails to the wind, Jesus went to the back of the boat. There He lay down and was soon fast asleep.

As the boat sailed across the Sea of Galilee, the wind blew stronger and stronger. This made the waves rise higher and higher. Soon the little boat was caught in a storm.

The storm grew worse with each passing minute. Great waves pounded against the boat, spilling more water into it than the disciples could take out.

"What can we do?" the disciples cried out. "We will drown!"

Some of the disciples worked frantically to bail out the water. Others worked to lower the sails from the strong wind.

But the boat was filling with so much water that they knew it would soon sink. The disciples were terrified. They had never seen the sea so violent before.

Then someone remembered Jesus. He was asleep in the back of the boat. They must wake Him and warn Him that the boat was going to sink.

Some of the disciples hurried to Jesus. "Master! Wake up!" they shouted. "Our boat is sinking!"

Jesus woke up and looked at the frightened faces of His disciples. Then He looked at the wild waves.

Quietly Jesus stood up and lifted His arms toward the sea. Then He shouted to the wind and waves, "Peace! Be quiet!"

The wind died down to a gentle breeze, and the waves began to rest. At once the storm was over, and the sea was calm again.

The disciples stared at Jesus as they watched Him command the wind and waves to be still. Now they feared Him more than the terrible storm. Never had they seen a man who could order the wind and waves to be still.

Jesus saw how afraid His disciples were. He gently asked them, "Why are you so frightened? Don't you believe in Me?"

The disciples were still very surprised at what they had seen. And they wondered at the way Jesus could make the wind and waves obey when no one else could.

WHAT DO YOU THINK?

What this story teaches: Jesus can do impossible things because He is God's Son.

1. Could any of your friends make the wind stop or the sea become calm? Why not?
2. Why was Jesus able to sleep in the storm? What did Jesus' disciples learn about Him? Why is it important to know that He is God's Son?
3. What are some things you want God's Son to do for you?

The Hundred-Pound Cream Puff

Mini pretended that she wasn't listening to Maxi and his friends. But she was.

"I can run faster than any of you guys," Pookie boasted.

That was true. Maxi and his friends knew that but didn't like to hear it.

"I can ride a bike without holding my hands on the handlebars," said another friend. "Can any of you guys do that?"

Nobody answered. Maxi had always wanted to try, but Mommi and Poppi had warned him that it could be dangerous and had asked him not to do it.

Big Bill Bluffalo flexed his muscles. "I can lick any of you guys in a fight," he bragged. "Anyone want to try to beat me?"

Nobody offered. They all knew that Big Bill could lick them. That's why they never got into a fight with him.

Big Bill looked at Maxi. "What can you do best, kid?" he asked. "Lift weights?"

Maxi's friends all laughed. They didn't think that Maxi could lift weights. Maxi's face became red. He certainly didn't think that was very funny.

Maxi didn't know what to say. He felt trapped. But he had to say something.

"Yeah," he answered. Maxi didn't know why he said that. Poppi had been doing a little weight-lifting for fun, but Poppi had said that Maxi was still a little young to do much with that.

"You CAN?" Maxi's friends all said at once.

Maxi gulped. Now he wished he hadn't said that. He felt trapped.

"How much can you lift, kid?" asked Big Bill. "A hundred pounds?"

"Yeah," Maxi answered.

"A HUNDRED POUNDS?" the friends all echoed.

Maxi gulped again. He knew that he should say then and there that he had made a mistake, that he really didn't mean to say that but it had come out of his mouth before he had thought.

"Cream puff!" Big Bill said, trying to trap Maxi more. "No problem, right kid?"

"Yeah," Maxi answered.

"This we have to see," said Pookie. "Come on, let's go!"

"I . . . well, I . . . my weights . . . ," Maxi stammered.

"Come on, let's go!" the friends all shouted.

Maxi and his friends trooped into the house and headed for the recreation room. "What's up?" Poppi asked.

"We're going to watch Maxi lift weights," said Big Bill. "He says he can lift a hundred pounds."

Poppi gulped now. He was still working on a hundred pounds!

"Cream puff!" was all Maxi could think now. He had almost convinced himself by this time that he could do it. Besides, he was praying that God would help him do it and get him out of this mess.

Maxi's friends gathered around closely as Maxi fastened a hundred pounds of weights together.

"Stand back!" Maxi called out to his friends.

The friends all stood back. Maxi seemed so sure of himself that they almost began to expect him to do it.

Maxi grabbed the rod that went through the weights. "Here we GO!" he shouted.

Maxi grunted and groaned as he tried to lift the weights from the floor. But nothing happened.

"Someone must have nailed them to the floor, kid," Big Bill snickered.

"Naw, Maxi just forgot to eat his spinach this morning," Pookie added.

Maxi's friends began to snicker and laugh at him. "A hundred pounds of cream puffs," they all said.

Maxi was still straining and groaning, trying to lift the hundred pounds as his friends all ran up the stairs laughing.

When they were gone, Maxi sat down by the weights and put his chin on his hands.

"Why?" he asked.

"Why what?" Poppi asked.

16

"Why did I ever say such a dumb thing," he said.

"Because we all sometimes start our mouth running before we put our brain in gear," said Poppi.

"But I prayed for God to help me lift them," Maxi added. "And He didn't."

"Then the hundred pounds of cream puffs helped you learn something about prayer," said Poppi.

"It did?" asked Maxi. "What?"

"Well," said Poppi. "If you were God would you help someone do something that might hurt him just because he bragged that he could do it?"

Maxi thought for a moment. "I guess I wouldn't," he answered. "But what can I say to my friends now?"

"That it's time to eat," said Poppi. "And when they laugh, laugh with them and tell them that it was fun to try."

Maxi ran to the kitchen. Before long he was carrying a tray of food to the table in the back yard where his friends were still laughing.

"Time for food!" Maxi called as he walked out with the tray.

"What are we having?" Big Bill shouted.

"CREAM PUFFS," said Maxi. "But not a hundred pounds of them!"

Maxi's friends all laughed. And Maxi laughed with them.

LET'S TALK ABOUT THIS

What this story teaches: We should not try to do things far beyond our ability. But if we do and others laugh at us, we should laugh with them and learn from our mistakes.

1. Do you ever say foolish things that you really did not want to say? Have you ever prayed for things which you really should not have?
2. What did Maxi learn when he did? What did Maxi learn to do when friends laughed at his mistakes?
3. What did you learn about prayer? What can you do when people laugh at your mistakes?

Sailing with Fishermen Friends

JOHN 21:1-14

Jesus' disciples were very quiet as they walked from Jerusalem back toward their home in Galilee. They were thinking of all that had happened in the past days.

They had come to Jerusalem with Jesus. They were going home without Him. He had been crucified in Jerusalem and had been buried. But He had risen from the tomb and showed Himself to many of His friends.

It seemed strange now to return to Galilee without Him. For three years these friends had gone everywhere with Him. They had watched Him heal the sick and help the blind see. They had seen Him quiet a storm and walk upon the water of their sea. Now they were alone.

"I'm going fishing!" said Simon Peter.

"We will go with you," said those disciples who were fishermen.

Peter and his fishermen friends had fished on the Sea of Galilee before they followed Jesus. Now that Jesus was gone, they would fish there again.

Soon the fishing boat and the net were ready, so the fishermen friends set sail on the sea. The sun was setting as they began to throw the fishing net into the water. How beautiful everything was, so different from the noise and danger they had found in Jerusalem.

At last the colors of the sunset faded in the west, and the stars began to twinkle. Again and again the fishermen threw out their net, hoping to catch some fish in it. Again and again they pulled it in empty.

All night long the fishermen worked. At last the first soft light of early morning appeared over the eastern hills. But still the fishermen friends had caught nothing. They felt very tired and discouraged.

"Let's try once more," one of the fishermen said. "If the net is empty, we'll go home."

This seemed a good idea to the others. The sun was now rising, sending a long orange and red path across the sea.

The fishermen picked up the great net to throw it. Suddenly they heard a voice calling from the nearby shore.

"Have you caught any fish?" the Man on the shore called to them.

"Not a one!" the fishermen answered. "We've worked all night and haven't caught one fish!"

"Throw your net on the right side of the boat," the Man called back. "There are fish over there."

How could a man on the shore know there were fish on the right side of the boat? It seemed foolish to try. But the fishermen were too tired and discouraged to argue. So why not throw the net once more on the right side of the boat?

The great net splashed into the water. As soon as it hit, the fishermen shouted with excitement.

"Fish! The water is filled with them!"

The fishermen rushed to the nets, hauling and tugging with all their might. Before long, the great net was tied safely behind the boat, filled with fish.

"Look at all those fish!" someone said.

Then the fishermen remembered the Man standing on the shore. All eyes turned in amazement toward him. Who was this man? How did he know about the fish?

Suddenly John realized who it was. "Peter," he said. "That's Jesus!"

Peter quickly put on his cloak and jumped into the shallow water along the shore, rushing to meet Jesus. The other fishermen brought their boat, and all their fish, to shore.

"Bring some of the fish you caught," Jesus told His friends.

Then they noticed a charcoal fire with bread and fish cooking on it. Before long, the fishermen friends were eating breakfast with Jesus.

As they ate breakfast together, the fishermen must have thought often of the great net filling with fish as it splashed over the right side of the boat. It was a miracle. Only Jesus could have done that. They were glad now that they had gone fishing, and that they had done it the way Jesus said they should.

WHAT DO YOU THINK?

What this story teaches: Jesus' way is always best.

1. Why do you think the disciples went fishing?
2. Why is it important to do things Jesus' way? Why not do everything your own way?
3. How might this story be different if the fishermen had not thrown the net on the right side of the boat, as Jesus said?

Indian War Parties and Fire-Breathing Dragons

"Wow!" Mini whispered softly.

Ruff cocked his sleepy head and let out a small woof. Even Tuff opened one eye, but then went back to her catnap. It would take more than a door slamming to disturb her catnap.

Mini knew that Maxi was angry when she heard the door slam and watched him stomp upstairs. "Maybe Maxi needs a friend," Mini thought, so she tiptoed upstairs and stood in Maxi's doorway.

"Hi, kid!" said Maxi. "Come on in."

Mini plopped into a chair and waited for Maxi to tell her what was wrong. If she asked first, Maxi would probably say that she was bugging him.

"Dumb Donald Doolittle!" Maxi grumbled.

"Big argument?" asked Mini.

"Yeah!"

"So? Forget it!"

"Are you kidding? Dumb Donald kept saying I told you so."

Mini smiled. She knew that Maxi might have said the same thing if he had won the argument. But that was different.

"I'll get even with him," Maxi said, looking a little fierce.

"Like what?" asked Mini.

"Like calling an Indian powwow. I'll bring all of the Indians in the tribe together tonight and we'll form a war party. At dawn we'll attack."

Mini's eyes grew wider. She could see the Indian war party riding down the street at dawn. She was almost ready to cheer Chief Maxi on until she saw some braves drag Donald from the house and tie him to a stake.

"Maxi."

"What?"

"I don't like the Indian war party. Can't you think of something else?"

"Sure. I'll bring Nimbo from his cave."

"Nimbo?"

"You know. The fire-breathing dragon. We'll sneak up to Donald's window by the light of the full moon.

23

Can't you see Dumb Donald running down the street with his pants on fire and Nimbo and me chasing him?"

Maxi chuckled when he saw that.

But Mini did not.

"Maxi."

"What?"

"I don't like fire-breathing dragons either. Can't you think of something else?"

Maxi thought for a minute. "I could jump in my fighter jet and drop water balloons on Donald as he runs for cover," he said. "I could even fill the balloons with purple ink. That would fix Dumb Donald. It would take a month for him to wash all that purple ink away."

Mini frowned. But Maxi went on talking.

"Then I would roar down into his back yard and grab my trusty sword and attack." Maxi grabbed his ruler and started slashing away at poor Donald, standing there covered with purple ink.

"Maxi."

"What?"

"Where did you get that sign over by the door?"

"Oh, my Sunday school teacher gave that to me a couple of weeks ago."

"What for?"

"I memorized the most Bible verses about love."

"Maxi."

"What?"

"What does the sign say?"

"What's the matter, kid? Can't you read? It says 'Jesus said, Love your enemies, too.'"

"Did Jesus say that?"

"Of course! The sign says so."

"Maxi."

"What?"

"I wonder what Jesus would say about Donald."

Maxi frowned. He tried to picture Jesus leading an Indian war party to Donald's house. But he just couldn't see Jesus doing that. Then he tried to picture Jesus riding a fire-breathing dragon down the street after Donald. But he couldn't see Jesus doing that either.

Maxi couldn't imagine Jesus dropping purple ink bombs on Donald or slashing at him with a trusty sword. Then Maxi looked back at the sign. What WOULD Jesus do?

"I . . . I guess Jesus would ask Donald to my party next week," Maxi said softly.

Mini smiled. "That's much better than Indian war parties and fire-breathing dragons," she said.

"Yeah," Maxi answered. "I'd better go call Dumb . . . I mean Donald right now."

LET'S TALK ABOUT THIS

What this story teaches: We will do things better and be happier with them if we do them Jesus' way.

1. Do you ever try to "get even" with friends when you're angry at them? What did Maxi want to do to "get even?" Why do you think Maxi and Mini were not happy with Maxi's way?

2. Why did Maxi change his mind about the war party and fire-breathing dragon? Why did Maxi and Mini both seem happier when Maxi decided to do things Jesus' way?

Sailing for Jesus

ACTS 2:38-47; 5:42; 8:5-6, 26-39; 10:1-48; 13:1-6

People everywhere were talking about Jesus. Thousands had become His followers and were telling their friends and neighbors about Him.

The people of Samaria believed when Philip told them about Jesus. Later, along a deserted road, Philip told an Ethiopian officer of the queen's court about Jesus. The man believed and went home to tell his people.

Some of the Roman soldiers believed, too. Peter was surprised when Cornelius, a Roman officer in Caesarea, accepted Jesus into his life.

The excitement went far beyond Jerusalem. To the north, in the city of Antioch, some Christians had started a church. There were important people in this church, including a man named Manaen, who had grown up with King Herod.

These Christians often met together to pray. One

day they were praying together when the Holy Spirit of the Lord spoke to them. The people listened carefully, for they wanted more than anything to do what would please God.

"Set Barnabas and Saul apart for some special work," the Holy Spirit told the people.

Barnabas and Saul had come back from a visit to Jerusalem and were working for Jesus there at Antioch. When the Christians at Antioch heard what the Holy Spirit wanted, they prayed about it.

As soon as the Christians at Antioch understood what the Holy Spirit wanted, they had a special meeting of the church. There they placed their hands on Barnabas and Saul.

"God is setting you apart for His special work," they said. "Go where He leads you. May God be with you."

Barnabas and Saul prayed for the Holy Spirit to lead them wherever He wanted them to go. After much prayer, they made their way to Seleucia, Antioch's seaport, where they boarded a ship for Cyprus. There they would tell the people about Jesus.

As the ship sailed for the island of Cyprus, where

Barnabas had lived many years before, the two men must have wondered what God would do through them. They could not know that God was sending them on a trip that would change the world.

Saul and Barnabas had set their sails to the wind for Jesus. There would be other trips like this one. And there would be hundreds, perhaps thousands, who would learn about Jesus through them.

WHAT DO YOU THINK?

What this story teaches: Jesus wants us to tell others about Him.

1. Why did Saul and Barnabas go on a long trip to another land? Why didn't they stay home and do what they wanted to do?
2. What would you do if God asked you to do some special work for Him? Would you do it? Why?
3. What special work can you do for God now?

With Sails to the Wind

"Poppi."

"Yes, Mini."

"Poppi, did Paul really sail far away on a big ship?"

"Of course."

"And did he go to many strange lands?"

"He did."

"And did he tell the people wherever he went about Jesus?"

"Wherever he went, Mini."

"Poppi."

"Yes, Mini."

"Could Maxi and I sail away to strange lands as Paul did?"

"How would you get there, Mini?"

"Oh, Maxi could make a strong ship, like a raft. It would be big enough for the two of us."

"To sail across the ocean?"

"Yes, Poppi. All the way across the ocean. We'd go to all the faraway lands."

"And what would you do when you got there?"

"We'd tell all the people about Jesus, just as Paul did. We'd tell them how Jesus loves them and how He wants them to love Him, too."

"Do you think they would listen to you?"

"Of course, Poppi. Maxi could preach and I'd sing and the crowds would gather around us as they did when Paul preached."

"Mini."

"Yes, Poppi."

"Not all of the people listened to Paul. Some of them threw big rocks at him. Some hated him because he told about Jesus."

"Maxi and I don't mind. We'd keep our ship ready so we could sail away to other places when some people get mean."

"Mini."

"Yes, Poppi."

"Why would you want to do this?"

"Poppi, many of these people have never heard about Jesus. My Sunday school teacher says so, and she knows everything."

"Everything?"

"Well, almost. Anyway, it would be fun to sail to faraway places, too, Poppi."

"Mini."

"Yes, Poppi."

"Is it just as much fun to tell people about Jesus when they don't live far away?"

30

"I . . . I guess so, Poppi. Like where?"

"Oh, like down the street or across town."

"But Poppi, do they need Jesus as much as the people far away?"

"Yes, Mini. They need Him just as much. And the people far away need Him just as much as our neighbors, too. They all need Him the same."

"Then why do people go far away to tell the people in other countries about Jesus? Why don't they stay home and talk to their neighbors?"

"Mini, if everyone stayed home, how would the faraway people hear about Jesus?"

"I . . . I guess they wouldn't, Poppi."

"And if everyone went far away, how would the people at home hear about Him?"

"They wouldn't, Poppi. So we need some people who will go far away and some people who will talk to the neighbors."

"Right, Mini, and some people who will talk to both."

"Poppi."

"Yes, Mini."

"Maybe Maxi and I can talk to our neighbor friends about Jesus now. Then later we can make our special ship and sail far away to tell people about Him."

"Hmmm. With sails to the wind for Jesus. I'm glad you want to do it for Jesus, Mini."

"Goodnight, Poppi."

"Goodnight, Mini."

LET'S TALK ABOUT THIS

What this story teaches: We should tell people near and far what Jesus has done for us.

1. What did Mini learn about the kinds of people who need Jesus? What did you learn?
2. Why do some people go far away to tell others about Jesus? Why do some people stay at home?

CHILDREN OF PROMISE

Angel in the Fire

JUDGES 13

The people of Israel were in trouble. Again and again they had worshiped strange gods. So the Lord punished them by letting the Philistines capture them.

For forty years the Philistines ruled over the people of Israel. This made the people of Israel very sad.

"What can we do?" some of the people asked.

"We can't fight the Philistines without a leader," some answered. "And we don't have a leader."

It was true. There was no great leader in Israel in those days. There was no one brave enough to lead them against the Philistines.

One day a woman of Israel was sitting alone in a field. Suddenly a man appeared and began to tell her strange things. The woman was sure that this man had come from God.

"You will soon have a son," the man told her.

"But how can this be?" the woman wondered. "I have never had a child. And I thought I never would have one."

But even though the woman wondered about this, she still believed the man who had come from God.

"You must never cut this boy's hair," the man said. "And you must never let him eat certain foods or take strong drink. He will do great work for God and will help Israel fight the Philistines."

The woman was so excited to hear this that she ran home to tell her husband Manoah. "I think this man was really the Angel of the Lord," the woman said.

Manoah prayed for God to send the man back again. "Let him return and tell us how to raise our new son," Manoah begged.

Not long after that, Manoah's wife was alone in the field again. Suddenly the Angel of the Lord appeared to her, so she hurried home to tell her husband.

Manoah ran to the field with his wife. "Are you the one who spoke to my wife the other day?" he asked.

"Yes," said the angel. "I am the one."

"Then please tell us how we should raise the new baby you have promised," Manoah asked.

"You must never let him eat certain foods or take strong drink," the angel said. "Also, your wife must not eat any food or drink that comes from the grapevine or certain foods. And she must never take strong drink."

Manoah wanted to be polite to the angel. "Will you stay and eat with us?" he asked.

"I will stay with you awhile," the angel answered. "But I will not eat. If you wish to bring something, you may offer a sacrifice to the Lord."

Manoah did not realize yet that this was the Angel of the Lord. So he asked the angel for his name. "When these things happen," Manoah explained, "we will want to honor you."

"Why do you ask for my name?" the angel asked. "It is a secret."

Manoah took meat and grain that he had brought and placed them on a rock as a sacrifice offering to the Lord. As the fire of the offering burned higher and higher, the Angel of the Lord went up toward heaven in the flames.

Manoah and his wife knew now that this was the Angel of the Lord. They kneeled down with their faces touching the ground.

"We have seen the Lord!" said Manoah. "We will die because we have looked at Him."

"No, the Lord would not do that," said Manoah's wife. "If He had planned for us to die, He would not have accepted our offering and promised us a child."

As time passed, Manoah and his wife did have a baby boy, just as the Lord had promised. They named him Samson. They knew that this son would someday lead their people against the Philistines.

"The Lord did all that He promised," Manoah and his wife often thought as they watched their baby. "Now we must do all that we promised Him."

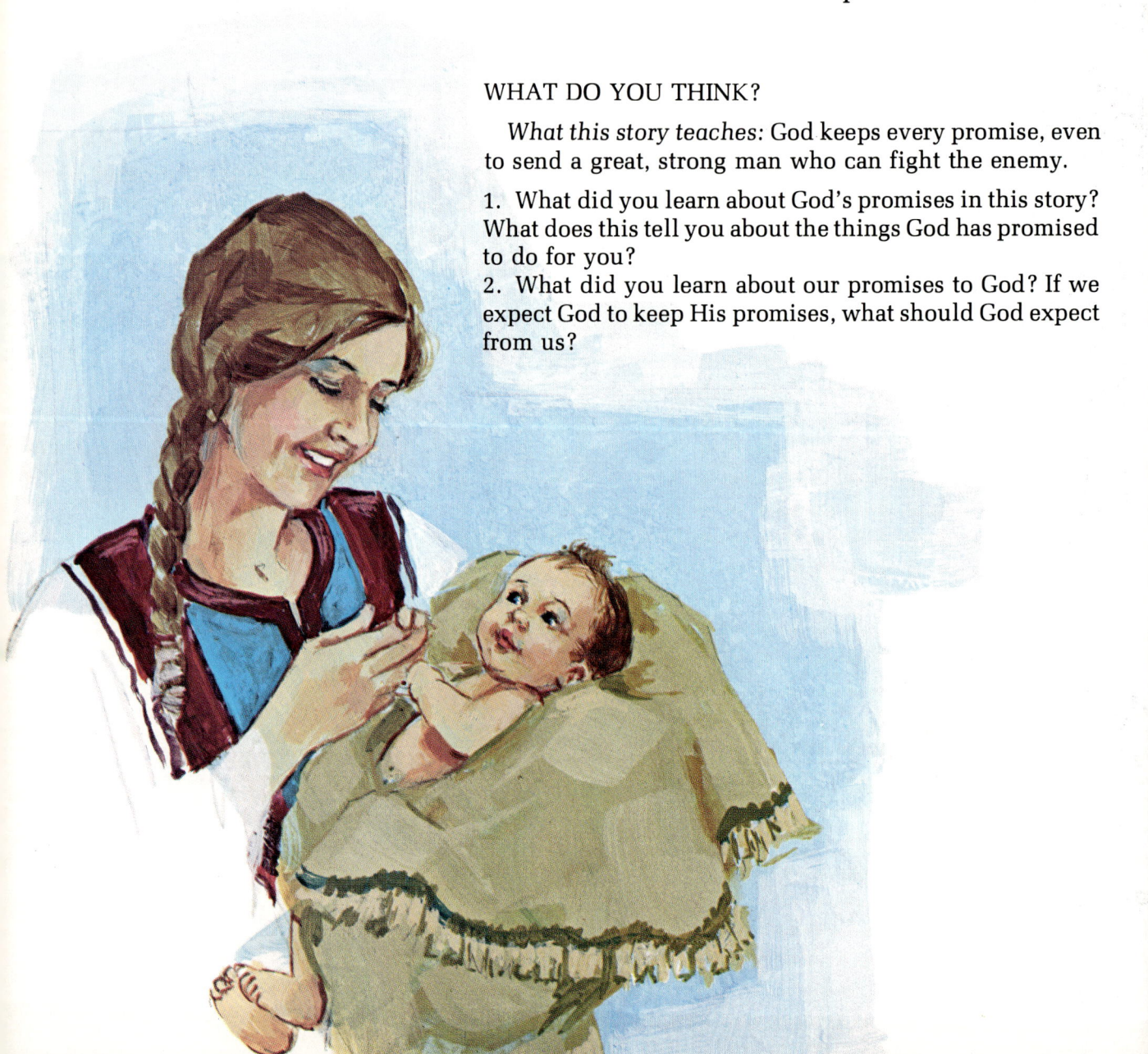

WHAT DO YOU THINK?

What this story teaches: God keeps every promise, even to send a great, strong man who can fight the enemy.

1. What did you learn about God's promises in this story? What does this tell you about the things God has promised to do for you?
2. What did you learn about our promises to God? If we expect God to keep His promises, what should God expect from us?

The Strongest Men in the World

"Poppi! Poppi!" Mini shouted, clapping her hands. "Aren't costume parties fun?"

Poppi smiled and nodded his head. He knew that Mini was excited about Maxi's costume party, even though Mini wasn't in a costume.

"Poppi, can you tell me what each costume is?" Mini asked.

"Why don't you see which ones you know first," said Poppi. "These are all cartoon characters and you know some of them."

Mini recognized Tigerman. Almost anyone would guess that. And she was sure that the silver one was Steelman.

"But what are the others?" Mini asked Poppi when she couldn't guess them.

"Well, I think that one is supposed to be Sooperman," said Poppi. "And the other one is Birdman."

"Poppi, what do all these men do?" Mini asked. "Why are there men like that?"

Poppi smiled. "They're not real men, of course," said Poppi. "They are all cartoon characters. People like to read about men who can do special things that we can't do. They like to pretend that these are the strongest men in the world."

"What can they do?" Mini asked.

"Tigerman can walk so quietly that even a cat can't hear him," said Poppi. "He can sneak up on criminals without a sound. When he's got them cornered, he can be as fierce as a tiger."

"Wow! I'm glad I'm not a criminal with him around," said Mini.

"Me, too," said Poppi. "Then there's Steelman. He's not quiet, but there's almost nothing that can hurt him. Bullets bounce off him like water drops."

37

"Is he always like that?" Mini asked.

"Oh, no. He's usually a science teacher in a school," said Poppi. "But when he takes a special formula, he becomes Steelman and goes out to fight crime."

"And what about Sooperman and Birdman?" Mini asked.

"Sooperman does everything a normal man does, but a hundred times greater," said Poppi. "He can hear, smell, and run a hundred times greater than I can. And he's a hundred times stronger. Birdman flies through the air when he's in his costume."

Mini thought for a moment. She had a frown on her face.

"Now what?" Poppi asked.

"I was just thinking," said Mini. "What kind of costume would God wear if we could see Him?"

"That's a good question, Mini," said Poppi. "But God is different from these men. They can do only certain things in a super way. But God can do anything. So He doesn't need a costume."

"Can He do more than Sooperman?" Mini asked.

"Yes," said Poppi. "There are three big words that tell about the things God can do. One word is OM-NIPOTENCE. It sounds like OM-NIP-PO-TENCE. That means God can do anything. He could even lift our whole world and throw it like a baseball if He wanted to."

"Wow!" said Mini. "None of those men could do that!"

"Right," said Poppi. "Now here's another word about God. It is OMNISCIENCE. It sounds like OM-NISH-ENCE. It means that God knows everything. He knows everything that was ever written in every book. He knows all about you and me, and everyone else. He even knows what will happen to us for the rest of our lives."

Mini frowned a little. "I guess I can't think of a costume that would fit God," she said. "What else can He do?"

"The third word is OMNIPRESENCE," said Poppi. "That sounds like OM-NI-PRES-ENTS. That means that God can be anywhere. He can even be in a million places at the same time. That's because He is everywhere at the same time."

Mini thought for a moment. "I wouldn't want to fight Him," said Mini. "I'm glad God is my friend."

"So am I," said Poppi. "So why don't we thank Him right now for being our friend and for letting us be His friend, too."

LET'S TALK ABOUT THIS

What this story teaches: We should be glad to be God's friend, for He is the greatest and strongest friend we can ever have.

1. Why should you be glad that God wants to be your friend? Why should you want to be His friend, too?
2. How is God greater than Samson? How is He greater than the special cartoon characters at Maxi's party?
3. We are God's special friends when we accept His Son Jesus as our Savior. Have you done that? Would you like to do that now? If you do, ask Him to forgive all your sins and become your Savior.

The Woman Who Kept Her Promise

1 SAMUEL 1:1-20

"Why don't you eat your dinner?" Elkanah asked his wife Hannah. "And why are you so sad? You must not cry like that."

"But I have no children," Hannah sobbed.

People sometimes made fun of a woman who had no children. They thought that God was punishing her for something. This made the woman even more sad.

Elkanah and Hannah had come to Shiloh to worship the Lord at the tabernacle, as they did each year. It should have been a very happy time. But the sight of other women and their children only reminded Hannah of her trouble. So it was not a happy time at all.

"Cheer up, Hannah," Elkanah told her. "I love you more than ten sons."

Hannah smiled at her husband. Of course he did! But she knew that they would both be happy to have a son.

Sad and alone, Hannah left Elkanah and the others at their camp and went over to the tabernacle to pray.

The tabernacle was a large tent where the people of Israel often went to pray and think about the Lord.

Hannah went to a quiet place and prayed silently to the Lord. "Oh, Lord, if You will give me a son, I will give him back to You to help You do Your work," she prayed.

Not far away, the old priest Eli watched. He could see Hannah's lips move but could not hear her praying.

"That woman is drunk!" Eli thought. Immediately he went to talk with her.

"You can't come into God's house that way," Eli told her.

Hannah felt sadder than ever. "I'm praying," she told Eli. Then she told him that she had been praying for something that she wanted very badly.

"God will answer your prayer," Eli said. "You may go and not feel sad."

This was such good news for Hannah. She had a song in her heart now, for she was sure that she would have a son.

One day Hannah's new son was born. It was the happiest day of her life. She named her son Samuel, which meant "I asked God for him."

When Samuel was old enough to leave home, Hannah took him to the tabernacle. "I am the woman who prayed for a son," Hannah told Eli. "Do you remember? Well, here is my son, Samuel. I promised the Lord that I would give my son to serve Him."

Hannah left young Samuel to help Eli care for God's house, the tabernacle. God had remembered her and helped her. Now Hannah kept her promise to Him.

WHAT DO YOU THINK?

What this story teaches: God expects His people to keep their promises.

1. What did Hannah want more than anything else? What did she promise that she would do if the Lord gave her a son?
2. What did Hannah do when the Lord answered her prayer? What does this story tell you about keeping promises to the Lord?

Too Many Promises

"The car wash will be fun, especially when we know how much money we can make for our missionary project," said Maxi's Sunday school teacher. "Be sure to come to the parking lot at Elm Street at 10:00 next Saturday morning. We'll wash from 10 until 11:00."

"I'll be there," said Maxi. "That will still give me the rest of the day for a hike."

But Maxi forgot about the car wash the next day when he and Pookie were walking home from school. Pookie and Maxi were good friends, so they often did things together.

"Hey, Maxi, have I got a neat job next Saturday at Pop's Sweet Shop!" said Pookie. "Pop said I could bring a friend and help clean up the storeroom. He said he will make us each a sooper-dooper chocolate sundae when we finish. How about it Maxi? It will only take an hour."

43

"That sounds great, Pookie," said Maxi. "I'll do it. That will still leave the rest of the day for a hike."

By Tuesday, Maxi forgot about his two promises. When Mini asked him to help her clean and oil her bike and pump up the tires, Maxi said "sure" without thinking. "It will only take about an hour," Maxi thought. "That will still give me the rest of the day for a hike."

Maxi was running out of the door on his way to school Wednesday morning when Mommi called to him. "Maxi, I'm going to clean the windows Saturday. How about giving me some help? It will only take about an hour."

"OK, Mommi," Maxi called back without thinking. "An hour isn't too bad. I'll still have the rest of the day for a hike."

Maxi forgot again on Thursday when Poppi asked him to help clean the garage. "An hour should do it," Poppi said.

"That's fine, Poppi, I'll be glad to help," said Maxi. "I'll still have the rest of the day for a hike."

On Friday Maxi promised another friend that he would help look for some pictures for a school project. It would only take an hour. That would still leave the rest of the day for a hike.

Just before breakfast on Saturday, Maxi began to pack a lunch. He was whistling cheerfully as Mommi, Poppi, and Mini came to the table for breakfast.

"What's the lunch for?" Mommi asked.

"I'm going on an all-day hike to the woods," said Maxi.

"But what about the windows?" asked Mommi. "You promised to help me for an hour."

"You're not forgetting the garage?" said Poppi. "You promised to help for an hour, too."

"And what about my bike, Maxi," said Mini. "You promised."

Suddenly Maxi remembered. "Oh, NO!" he said. "Now I remember! I also promised Pookie that I'd help him for an hour at Pop's Sweet Shop. Then Maxi remembered his promise to help with the car wash and to help his friend look for pictures.

44

"Six promises!" Maxi groaned. "How can I do it?"

While Maxi groaned some more, Poppi read the story about Samuel's birth from the new Muffin Family book. He read how Hannah kept her promise, even when it meant giving her son to the Lord.

"What does this story tell you about keeping promises to the Lord?" Poppi read when the story was finished.

Maxi sat up in his chair. "Does it really ask that in our book?" he asked.

"Look for yourself," said Poppi.

"I . . . I guess if Hannah could give up so much to keep her promises, I can give up a few hours to keep mine," said Maxi. "So maybe I'd better figure how I'm going to do it."

Maxi took a piece of paper and began writing. From 8:30 until 9:30 help Mommi with windows. Go to parking lot. From 10 until 11, work with Sunday school car wash. Go downtown. From 11:30 until 12:30 work at Pop's Sweet Shop. From 12:30 until 1, eat chocolate sundae. Come home. From 1:30 until 2:30 help Mini with bike. From 2:30 until 3:30 help Poppi with garage. Go to friend's house. From 4 until 5 help friend look for pictures.

Maxi looked at his paper. Then he wrote "Take hike next Saturday. I promise! Maxi."

Then Maxi hurried off to keep his promises.

LET'S TALK ABOUT THIS

What this story teaches: We should keep every promise that we make to God and others, no matter what that costs us.

1. What did Maxi learn from Hannah about keeping promises? Why do you think he felt he should keep his promises to friends and family, just as Hannah kept her promises to the Lord?
2. Why is it important to keep your promises to friends and family? Why is it important to keep your promises to the Lord?

The Miracle Child

LUKE 1:5-25, 57-66

It was a special day for the old priest Zacharias, for it was his turn to offer incense in The Holy Place. Many years would pass before Zacharias could do this again. Perhaps by that time he would be too old.

Quietly Zacharias walked past the crowds of people in the Temple, God's house. At last he stepped into the quiet room called The Holy Place. He was alone there, for no one else could enter.

Suddenly Zacharias was startled, for he saw that someone else was in the room with him. The other person did not really look like a man, but like an angel.

"Who . . . who are you?" Zacharias whispered. His voice trembled as he spoke, for the old priest was afraid.

"You must not be afraid of me," the angel answered. "I have come to bring you good news. You and your wife Elizabeth will have a baby. You will name him John. When this baby is grown, he will do great work for God."

"But we are too old," Zacharias protested. "We cannot have a baby now."

Then the angel said, "I am Gabriel, God's messenger. He has sent me to tell you this good news. But since you did not believe me, you will not be able to talk until your son is born."

46

When the angel finished speaking, he was gone. Zacharias was alone again in the room, puzzled and frightened by the things he had heard.

At last Zacharias finished offering the incense to the Lord and walked from The Holy Place. The people who waited outside wondered why it had taken so long for him to finish. They did not know about the angel. Zacharias could not tell them, either, for he could not speak. But the people could see that something strange and wonderful had happened to him.

The days passed until the time when the child was born. Neighbors and friends gathered to share the excitement. On the eighth day after the child's birth, it was time to name him.

"Why don't you name him for his father?" some of the neighbors suggested.

"No, we will name him John," Elizabeth answered.

"But none of your family has that name," they argued. "Let's ask Zacharias what he thinks."

Of course Zacharias could not speak, so he motioned for someone to bring him a writing tablet. When they did, he wrote on it, "His name will be John."

As soon as Zacharias wrote that, he could speak. Immediately he began praising God for all that had happened.

The friends and neighbors could see by now that this child was a miracle, for God had sent him in a strange and wonderful way. Before long the news of this baby spread throughout the countryside.

Elizabeth and Zacharias watched with wonder as the child grew. What great work did God have for him? They must wait to see. But they often thanked God for the special son whom He had promised when they were too old to have a baby.

WHAT DO YOU THINK?

What this story teaches: God can do anything, even though some things may be hard to believe.

1. Why was it hard for Zacharias to believe the angel's message? What happened when he did not believe?
2. Did God's promise come true? This child became John the Baptist. What else do you know about him?

A Walk Through the Woods

"I'm so glad you can go with me on my hike, Poppi," said Maxi. "That makes it a special hike!"

"I'm glad, too," said Poppi.

Ruff was glad that Maxi and Poppi had taken him along. He liked to run through the woods and bark at squirrels. Sometimes the squirrels barked back at Ruff in their own little squirrel bark.

Maxi looked for new things in the woods whenever he went on a hike. So he was excited when Ruff sniffed a big anthill.

"Look at all those busy ants," Maxi said. "How can they work so hard on a beautiful Saturday morning? It's much more fun to take a hike in the woods."

Poppi laughed. "Not if you're an ant! See how much fun they're having, even when they carry those big things on their backs."

Poppi and Maxi sat down near the anthill to watch. Ruff couldn't just sit there, so he went to find a squirrel.

Maxi began to ask questions about the trees and other wonderful things in the woods. He was sure that Poppi was the smartest man in the world because he could answer so many questions. But Poppi always thought he must be one of the dumbest men in the world because there were so many questions he couldn't answer.

"Poppi, how can such a big tree come from such a small acorn?" Maxi asked.

"It doesn't happen all at once," said Poppi. "God makes it grow a day at a time."

"But where does all the stuff to make the tree come from?" asked Maxi. "God doesn't get it all from a little acorn, does He?"

Poppi laughed. "No, Maxi, He doesn't. He mixes some rain and sunshine with the acorn and adds some food from the soil."

"But how can He do it?" Maxi asked. "You can't do that, can you, Poppi? And you can do almost anything."

"He can do it because He's God," said Poppi. "And God can do anything."

Maxi wasn't sure that Poppi had answered his question but he decided not to say any more about it now. Instead, he would look at some of the other wonderful things in the woods.

"Poppi, just look at all those big rocks over there," said Maxi. "Where did they come from?"

"God put them there," said Poppi.

"But how could God lift such BIG rocks?" Maxi asked. "You couldn't lift those, could you, and you're my Poppi?"

Poppi smiled again. "No, I couldn't lift those rocks," he said. "I couldn't even lift one of them."

"But you can do almost anything," said Maxi.

"No, Maxi, not almost anything," said Poppi. "I can do a few things that Poppis can do. But God can do so much more."

Then Poppi told Maxi some of the things that God can do that a Poppi can't do. "He can paint a sunrise or sunset and make the moon rise at night. He can give life to a new baby or a new pony and no Poppi can do that. And God can make the wind blow and the flowers come from tiny seeds."

"Is God much bigger than you are, Poppi?" Maxi asked.

Poppi bent over the anthill and pointed to an ant carrying a little white load on its back. "Can you pick up that thing the ant is carrying, Maxi?" Poppi asked.

"I could pick up a thousand of them," said Maxi.

"Maybe ten thousand," said Poppi.

Poppi picked up a little stone about the size of a marble. He tossed it near the anthill. "Do you think an ant could carry this on his back?"

Maxi looked at the ant. Then he looked at the stone. "Oh, no, Poppi. It's much, much too big."

Poppi picked up the little stone and tossed it to Maxi. "It doesn't feel very big to you, does it?" he asked. "See how far you can throw it."

Maxi threw the stone all the way to the big tree.

50

A SLAVE WHO RULED THE LAND

But Reuben, the oldest brother, did not like that idea. Since he was the oldest, it would be his fault if something happened to Joseph.

"No, we must not kill our own brother," Reuben told the others. "Let's throw him into that dry well over there instead."

So when Joseph arrived, the brothers grabbed him and tore off his beautiful cloak. Then they threw him into the well, and they sat down to eat.

But while the others ate, Reuben went into the fields to look at the sheep. He thought he would come back when his brothers were gone and pull Joseph from the old well.

Suddenly Judah, one of the older brothers, looked up from his supper. "There's a caravan coming," he said. It was a caravan of traders, taking their goods to Egypt.

"Let's sell Joseph to the traders," said Judah. "Then we will not need to kill him."

The others liked this better than killing their own brother, so they agreed. When the caravan arrived, they pulled Joseph from the old well and sold him for twenty pieces of silver.

Later that evening Reuben came back to pull Joseph from the well. But when he looked in, he saw that the well was empty.

55

The Jealous Brothers

GENESIS 37

"Joseph, will you asked. Joseph nodde to help his father.

"Your older broth said Jacob. "Please g is well with them a

Joseph put on a be given him and went Joseph came across they began to gruml

"Look at him!" th than we are."

The brothers wer some dreams which The dreams seemed brothers would bow only that, but the b important people w thought Joseph was

"Let's kill him!" "We can put some bl think that a wild an

Reuben began to tear his clothes when he found that Joseph had been sold. "Now what do I do?" he cried out.

The other brothers killed a goat and splashed some of its blood on Joseph's torn cloak. Then they took it back to their father.

"Is this Joseph's cloak?" they asked. "We found this while we were in the fields."

Old Jacob took the torn cloak in his hands and looked at it. "Yes," he sobbed. "It is Joseph's cloak. He has been torn to pieces by a wild animal."

Jacob put on some old cloth and sat in his tent to mourn. "I'm so sad that I could die," he cried out. The other sons tried to comfort him, but Jacob was too sad.

Now the brothers were sorry for what they had done. But it was too late. Their jealousy had hurt their brother. It had hurt their father. And it would hurt them, too, as they watched their father suffer, but would not tell him the truth.

WHAT DO YOU THINK?

What this story teaches: Jealousy hurts God and those we love.

1. Why were Joseph's brothers jealous?
2. What evil thing did they do because they were jealous?
3. Who got hurt because of this? Joseph? Jacob? How did the older brothers get hurt by selling Joseph?

Tuff and Taffy

Mini's eyes sparkled as she ran into the house with a ball of fur in her arms. But Mommi's eyes did not sparkle when she saw what the ball of fur was.

"Mini, where did you get that cat?" Mommi asked. "And why are you bringing it here?"

"Oh, Mommi, Terry said someone dropped it at her house last night and she can't keep it. Please, may I keep it here?" Mini asked.

"But Mini! We already have a cat. What would Tuff think?"

"She would love it!"

"Even if she did, Poppi and I wouldn't. One cat is enough!"

"Please, Mommi, may I keep it tonight?"

"Tonight only. Then we will take it to the Humane Society tomorrow."

Mini took the new cat into the living room where Tuff was sleeping. She put the cat in front of Tuff and woke her.

"Look, Tuff! A new friend for you."

Tuff arched her back and growled. The new cat arched her back and growled, too.

"Tuff! Be nice to this taffy-colored cat!" Mini said sternly.

Mini picked up the new cat and cuddled it in her arms. Tuff rubbed against Mini as if to say "Look at me! I'm here!"

"You will be nice to Taffy, won't you?" Mini said, almost scolding Tuff. But when Mini put Taffy down Tuff arched her back again and growled.

"Tuff! Shame on you!" said Mini.

Mini ran to the kitchen to tell Mommi about Tuff. As soon as she ran through the doorway, Tuff growled at Taffy. Taffy did not like this, so she growled back. Then Tuff crouched down and before Taffy knew what had happened Tuff jumped on her and began to fight.

Taffy let out a big "YEOWWW" and took off across the room with Tuff after her. By this time Taffy was frightened. She wanted to climb something but there was nothing to climb except the living room drapes.

So she climbed them!

Tuff sat below the drapes, waiting for Taffy to let go. When she did, Taffy took long pieces of the drapes with her in her claws. Then she ran across the room again with Tuff after her.

Mommi and Mini rushed into the room just as Taffy made a flying leap across the sofa. But when she tried to jump to another chair, Taffy landed KER-PLOP in the aquarium, just as Ruff had done another time.

"TAFFY!" Mini shouted as she rushed to fish a very wet cat from the aquarium.

By this time Taffy was so frightened that she tried to claw Mini. But Mommi rushed over with a towel, and they quickly dried poor Taffy and wrapped the towel around her to keep her from running more.

That night Taffy slept in a box that Poppi fixed for her in the garage. Tuff slept in her basket.

After dinner, Poppi read the Bible story "The Jealous Brothers" in the Muffin Family book *With Sails to the Wind*. Mini thought of Tuff when Poppi asked some questions about Joseph's jealous brothers and how they hurt Joseph, their father, and themselves with their jealousy.

"Was Tuff like Joseph's jealous brothers?" Mini asked.

Poppi thought for a moment. "In some ways, she was," he answered. "Tuff couldn't stand to see you show so much love to Taffy. Joseph's brothers couldn't stand to see their father show so much love to Joseph."

"Was Tuff wrong? Should she be punished?" Mini asked.

"That's where Tuff is different from Joseph's brothers," said Poppi. "They knew that they would hurt these other people. Tuff is a cat. She didn't know that she would hurt you or Mommi. So she did what any other jealous cat would do."

"Poppi."

"Yes, Mini."

"Does jealousy always hurt others?"

"Usually. A jealous person wants what someone else has. He's willing to fight for it, too. Then someone gets hurt. The jealous person usually hurts someone he loves. He often hurts God, too."

"Then Tuff and Taffy taught me something I needed to know," said Mini.

"What's that, Mini?" Poppi asked.

"That I shouldn't be like a jealous Tuff cat or I might hurt someone I love. I might even hurt God."

Poppi smiled. "Hmmm," he said. "Tuff and Taffy's terrible tiff taught two terrific things!"

Then Poppi and Mini laughed together.

LET'S TALK ABOUT THIS

What this story teaches: We must try to avoid jealousy so that we do not hurt God and those we love.

1. How was Tuff like Joseph's jealous brothers? How was she different?
2. What did Mini learn from Tuff and Taffy? Can you think of any times when you have been jealous? Did you hurt someone with your jealousy? What will you remember the next time you are jealous?

59

Slave in a Strange Land

GENESIS 39

As the caravan of traders came closer to Egypt, Joseph wondered what would happen to him. His mind whirled with strange thoughts. Why did his own brothers sell him to these traders to become a slave? Who would buy him? And what kind of work would he have to do? Would he be whipped and beaten as he worked under the hot sun?

"But the Lord is with me," Joseph said to himself many times. "I know He will take care of me."

When the traders had sold their goods, they took Joseph to the slave market. Egyptians who wanted slaves would come there to buy.

Joseph watched the Egyptians who came to buy. Which one would be his new master? Would it be the man over there with the hard, evil face? Or the one with the kind face? He was sure that the Lord would give him the right kind of master. Joseph must have prayed many times for the Lord to be with him and help him.

Suddenly the man with the kind face came toward Joseph. He watched as Joseph stood tall and fearless. He knew that Joseph was no ordinary slave.

"I will buy him," the kind man said to the traders. "He will make a fine servant for my household."

Joseph worked hard for the kind man, whose name was Potiphar. Whatever Potiphar asked, Joseph did it quickly. He even did many good things which Potiphar did not expect him to do.

Potiphar noticed how things had changed in his household since Joseph came. He saw that Joseph prayed to the Lord and did what pleased the Lord. Soon Potiphar knew that the Lord was with Joseph, helping him do his work, even though he was a slave.

One day Potiphar had a talk with Joseph. "Things have gone well since you came," he said. "So I am placing you over all my household."

The Lord continued to do many good things for Potiphar because of Joseph. His crops grew better and his flocks grew larger than they had ever been before.

Once more Potiphar talked to Joseph. "The Lord is with you," he said. "I am now placing you over everything I own."

"Surely the Lord is taking care of me," Joseph thought. "He has done so many good things for me."

But Potiphar's wife had fallen in love with Joseph. One day she saw Joseph alone.

"Come here and sit with me," she whispered.

"No, I can't do that," Joseph answered. "Potiphar has done so much for me. How could I do this to him?"

But Potiphar's wife kept trying day after day. One day when they were alone, she grabbed Joseph's cloak. Joseph ran from the room.

When Potiphar came home that night, his wife told lies about Joseph. She said that Joseph had tried to hurt her.

Potiphar was angry now. He had Joseph thrown into prison.

It was dark and lonely in the prison. Joseph often sat there, thinking of all that had happened to him. The Lord had been with him at his home back in Canaan. He had taken care of him when he came to Egypt as a slave, giving him a good master. And He had been with him while he served Potiphar.

"Will the Lord still be with me here?" Joseph must have wondered. As he thought and prayed about it, Joseph became more certain than ever that the Lord was with him and would take care of him, even in the prison in Egypt.

WHAT DO YOU THINK?

What this story teaches: God expects us to be faithful to Him and to those we love.

1. How do you think Joseph felt as he was taken to Egypt as a slave? What difference did it make that the Lord was with him?
2. While Joseph was a slave, what happened that showed that the Lord was with him? How do you think this story would have changed if Joseph had cursed God instead of trusting Him?

The Tea Party
Under the Tree House Party

Maxi invited Pookie and Big Bill to a tree house party. Mini invited her friends to a tea party. The problem was that Mini's tea party was under Maxi's tree house where he was having his tree house party.

Mini and her friends were not really drinking tea. It was pretend tea.

Maxi and his friends were not really having a party. It was more like a club meeting.

When Mini and her friends said something funny all of them giggled. And when girls giggle, boys in tree houses above them begin to get ideas.

"I can't believe it!" said Big Bill.

"Can't believe what?" asked Maxi.

"I can't believe those dumb girls."

"What about them?"

"That they would have their dumb little party down there."

"Why not?"

"Under a tree house filled with boys?"

Maxi looked puzzled. "Why not?"

Big Bill smiled a mischievous kind of smile.

"Well, I can think of several good reasons," he said. "Like water balloons or pepper that float down on a table from a tree house. Or the sky could rain down a pitcher of pink drink. Wow! Wouldn't that make a nice little tea party interesting?"

"You wouldn't dare do that!" Maxi argued.

"Heh. Heh. Heh. Wouldn't I?" said Big Bill. "What do you say, Pookie?"

Pookie was always chicken around Big Bill. He was afraid of Bill. So he gulped and nodded his head yes.

"Well, you can't do that to my little sister," said Maxi. "And that's that!"

Big Bill slapped his leg with his hand and laughed. "Pookie, did you hear what I heard?" he sneered. "This kid is actually trying to protect his little sister. You could wrap my sister in cookie dough and bake her in the oven and I wouldn't care. We're always fighting."

63

"Well, Mini and I aren't always fighting," Maxi argued. "Just sometimes. You leave her alone. If you don't want to do that, you can go home."

Maxi sounded so tough that Big Bill knew he meant it. Since he couldn't spoil the tea party, Bill thought he would make fun of Maxi.

"Pookie, what do you call a guy who sides with girls?" he croaked.

Pookie shook his head. He didn't want to make fun of Maxi. Maxi was his best friend. But he didn't want to get Big Bill angry at him. Bill was too big.

"He's a SISSY!" Bill hung onto the word as if he was wrapping it around Maxi's neck. "Now come on kid, let's get some water balloons and give them a little toss so all your friends at school don't hear that you've been a SISSY!"

"No way!" said Maxi. "Like I said, Bill, if you don't want to leave Mini and her friends alone, you can go home."

"OK, SISSY," said Bill, "I'll just do that."

With that, Bill climbed down the ladder and headed home. But on the way he gave Mini's table a big bump and spilled her pretend tea over the table.

"That's for having a SISSY for a brother," said Big Bill.

That night at the dinner table Mini could see that Maxi was sad. "Why did Big Bill call you a sissy?" she asked.

Poppi coughed a little fake cough and Mommi looked over her glasses at Mini. They thought that Mini was going to start an argument.

"Oh, Big Bill didn't like something I said," Maxi answered.

"Like what?"

Poppi cleared his throat and Mommi looked over her glasses again. "Really, Mini!" they both said.

"That's OK," said Maxi. "I just told him he could go home."

"Why?" Mini prodded.

"Because he wanted to drop water balloons on your tea party," said Maxi. "I told him he could go home. So he called me a sissy for saying that."

Poppi put his fork down and looked at Maxi. "Seems to me that Joseph settled that argument," he said.

"Who?" Maxi asked.

"Joseph, in the Bible. Joseph was faithful to God and Potiphar, even when it hurt him," said Poppi. "It takes a real man to do that. You were like Joseph today, for you were faithful to your family even when it hurt."

Maxi didn't look sad now. He had a big smile on his face. "Do you really think so, Poppi?" he asked.

"Yes, sir!" said Poppi. "Now stand up. We'd each like to come and shake your hand for being a strong man like Joseph."

Maxi felt a little strange when his family shook hands with him. But it was fun having Poppi tell him he was a man.

LET'S TALK ABOUT THIS

What this story teaches: We should be faithful to God and those we love.

1. Why did Poppi call Maxi a man instead of Big Bill? How was Maxi like Joseph?
2. Do you build up your family to others or tear it down? Do you build up your brothers or sisters to others or do you tear them down? How can you be more like Maxi and Joseph?

65

A Strange Day in Joseph's Life

GENESIS 40:1—41:46

Day after day, week after week, Joseph sat in the dark and lonely Egyptian prison. Often he must have wondered why. Why didn't Potiphar believe him? Why did God leave him there? He had tried to do what God wanted, and now he was in prison for it.

But Joseph kept on trusting God to do the right thing. He knew that God had taken care of him so far and would keep on doing it.

One day two important men were put into prison with Joseph. Pharaoh, the king, had become angry at them, so that was the way he punished them.

Not long after they came to the prison, these men had some strange dreams and told them to Joseph. Then God helped Joseph know what each dream meant.

"You will be taken from prison soon to work with the king," Joseph told one man. "When you do, remember me."

Then Joseph spoke to the other man. "Your dream says that you will be put to death in three days."

Not long after that, the first man was taken from prison and sent back to work with the king. The other man was put to death, just as Joseph had said.

But the first man forgot to tell the king about Joseph. He forgot to tell how Joseph knew the meaning of his dream.

Two years went by, and Joseph stayed in prison, wondering if he would ever get out. But one night Pharaoh had a strange dream. It was so strange that he called all of his magicians and wise men.

"Tell me the meaning of my dream," Pharaoh demanded. But the magicians and wise men could not.

Then the man who had been in prison remembered Joseph. "There is a man who can tell you the meaning of your dream," he said. The man told Pharaoh about Joseph and how he had told the meaning of his dream.

Pharaoh sent some men to the prison to get Joseph. Of course, Joseph was very surprised.

"Me?" he asked. "Pharaoh, king of Egypt, wants to talk to me? Why?"

"We don't know," said the men. "But hurry and get dressed and shave. We must not keep the king waiting."

Joseph shaved and dressed in the clean clothing the men gave him. Then he hurried with them to meet Pharaoh.

"Last night I had two strange dreams," Pharaoh explained to Joseph. "While I stood on the bank of the Nile River, seven fat cows came up from the river. They were followed by seven skinny cows, who ate the seven fat cows. But they were still skinny."

Pharaoh looked worried as he spoke to Joseph. "I awoke for a while," he said. "When I went back to sleep, I dreamed about seven good heads of grain on a stalk. From the same stalk came seven withered heads of grain. The withered heads ate the good heads of grain. I called for my magicians and wise men. But no one could tell me the meaning of these dreams."

"The dreams both have the same meaning," Joseph said to Pharaoh. "God is telling you that you will have good crops for seven years. Then you will have famine for seven years. Your people will eat everything you have saved during the good years."

"But what can we do?" Pharaoh wondered.

"Find a wise man to gather grain for you during the good years," said Joseph. "When the famine comes, you will have food to eat."

Pharaoh talked with his officers about Joseph's plan. Then he spoke to Joseph.

"Who is wiser than you?" he said. "I will place you over all the land of Egypt. I am the only one greater than you."

Pharaoh gave Joseph his ring and dressed him in beautiful clothes. He gave Joseph a fine chariot and arranged for him to marry a beautiful girl.

In the morning, Joseph had been a slave in prison. By evening, he was governor of all Egypt.

"God works in strange ways," Joseph must have thought as he rode away in his new chariot. But Joseph knew that God had been with him—in prison or in the presence of Egypt's king.

WHAT DO YOU THINK?

What this story teaches: God wants us to tell others, even those in high places, that we belong to Him.

1. How could Joseph know that God was with him, both in times of trouble or in good times?
2. Was Joseph more faithful to God one time than another? How did he show his faithfulness to God when he talked to the king of Egypt?
3. How had God prepared Joseph for his new responsibilities?

A Time for Yes or No

"Mommi! Poppi! Guess what?"

That always caught Mommi's and Poppi's attention. But they never knew what to guess.

"What is it, Maxi?" they asked.

"My principal has recommended me for a weekend job," Maxi panted. "At the NEWSPAPER OFFICE!"

"Are you sure?" Poppi asked.

"Sure I'm sure!" Maxi beamed. "My principal is a friend of Mr. Pressly, the publisher. Mr. Pressly said he wants a boy he can trust to come down one day each week and help them with a special project."

"What kind of a project?" Poppi asked.

"They're making a book called School Scrapbook of Yesterday," said Maxi. "It will show school kids and events from old newspapers."

Poppi smiled. "Maybe they will have some of our old school pictures in it," he said. "That will be great."

"But what does Mr. Pressly want you to do?" asked Mommi.

Maxi wiped some of the smile from his face. "Well, it's not a big job," he said. "Just helping to sort the files of pictures and get them in order. It's a favor to my principal."

"That's wonderful," said Poppi. "We're proud of you. To think you are the one the principal recommended. When do you see Mr. Pressly?"

"Right now!" said Maxi. "I'll clean up and run to the newspaper office as fast as I can."

Maxi scrubbed and rubbed and polished and combed. Before long he was on his way to see Mr. Pressly.

"Well, well," said Mr. Pressly. "So this is the young man George recommended. Come in, Maxi. You must be quite a fine young man."

Maxi thought he was blushing a little when he heard that. But he didn't want to blush. Big Bill always said that girls blush and men don't.

"Thank you, sir," said Maxi. "I'm so glad you asked me to come down."

Mr. Pressly showed Maxi the picture files and told him how it would be done. Then he showed him around the office.

"Now Maxi, you can start this Sunday morning," said Mr. Pressly.

"Sunday morning?" Maxi asked. He was sure Mr. Pressly could see the disappointment on his face.

"Yes," Mr. Pressly answered. "The men and women working on this project are doing it as extra work on Sunday mornings, so that's when you will need to come, too.

Maxi was quiet for a moment. He wasn't sure how to answer Mr. Pressly, but he would try.

"Is something wrong?" Mr. Pressly asked.

"Well, sir, you see," Maxi stammered, "I do want the job, very very much. But Mommi and Poppi and Mini and I go to Sunday school and church every Sunday morning. I . . . I just don't think Jesus would want me to stop doing that for this job."

Mr. Pressly looked shocked. "You would really give up the job you want for that?" he asked.

"Yes, sir," Maxi answered. "But thank you for letting me talk with you."

70

Maxi looked so sad when he turned to leave. Mr. Pressly was quiet as he watched Maxi close the office door behind him and walk toward the front of the building. Maxi was almost outside when he heard Mr. Pressly calling him.

"Wait!" called Mr. Pressly. "Come back."

Mr. Pressly held out his hand when Maxi came back. "I want to shake your hand, young man," he said. "That was a very brave thing you did. You're just the one I'm looking for."

"But I can't take this job, sir," Maxi answered.

"Not this job!" said Mr. Pressly. "I have a MUCH BETTER one for you. You gave me a great idea for a new feature in the newspaper each week. School Scrapbook Today! And YOU will be the junior reporter. You can do it after school two afternoons each week. How about it?"

"Yes, SIR!" said Maxi.

LET'S TALK ABOUT THIS

What this story teaches: We are happier when we are not ashamed of God, even to people in high places.

1. How was Maxi like Joseph, when Joseph went before Pharaoh? What did each have to lose by being faithful to God? What did each gain?
2. If you had been Joseph, would you have said what he said about God? If you had been Maxi, would you have said what he said?
3. How might this story have been different if Maxi had agreed to work on the first job?

A Time to Forgive

GENESIS 42:1—45:16

For seven years the crops in Egypt were very good. People had more grain than they needed, so Joseph put this grain into Pharaoh's storehouses. God had warned that a great famine was coming, and Joseph knew that this grain would keep the people from starving.

At last the seven good years came to an end. The crops began to wither and die. There was no more grain for the people to eat.

"We must have food!" the people cried out.

"Go to Joseph," Pharaoh told them. "He will give you food to eat."

The people of Egypt went to Joseph, and he gave

them grain to eat. As the famine grew worse, it went beyond Egypt into the surrounding lands.

In Canaan, Jacob's family had little to eat, too, for the famine had reached their land. One day Jacob spoke to his ten oldest sons.

"Go down to Egypt and buy grain for us," he said.

The brothers were afraid when he mentioned Egypt. They remembered Joseph and the traders who took him there as a slave. But there was no other place where they could buy food, so they saddled their donkeys and left for Egypt.

"We have come to buy grain," they said when they arrived in Egypt. "Who will sell it to us?"

"The governor!" some people answered.

When the brothers came before the governor, they did not know that he was Joseph. And Joseph did not tell them.

"We have come to buy grain," they said.

"No!" Joseph answered. "You are spies." Joseph wanted to test them, to see if they were sorry they had sold him as a slave.

The brothers quickly told about their family. "We have a younger brother and a father at home," they said. "And one of our brothers is dead." They were talking about Joseph, thinking that he had died in Egypt.

Joseph pretended that he was angry and made his brothers go to prison for three days. It may have been the same prison where he had stayed for more than two years. Now they would know what it was like to be in prison in Egypt.

At the end of three days, Joseph talked with his brothers again. "One of you will stay in prison until the others come back with your youngest brother," he said. "Then I will know that you are telling me the truth."

When the brothers reached home and told Jacob what the governor said, old Jacob was hurt and angry. "No! You must not take Benjamin to Egypt," he said. "He and Joseph were the only sons of my beloved wife Rachel. Now Rachel and Joseph are both dead. I cannot lose Benjamin, too."

But the days passed and the grain was soon gone. "We must take Benjamin, or we cannot buy more grain and free Simeon from prison," the brothers told Jacob.

So the brothers took money and gifts for the governor and left for Egypt with Benjamin. When they came before Joseph, they bowed down, just as Joseph had dreamed that they would many years before.

Joseph tested his brothers in other ways, until he was sure that they were sorry they had sold him as a slave. At last he could keep his secret no longer.

"I am your brother Joseph!" he told them. "You sold me as a slave. But you must not be angry at yourselves, for God has sent me here to save us from the famine."

The brothers were so surprised that they could not speak. They were even more surprised that Joseph forgave them for selling him as a slave.

Joseph threw his arms around his brothers and wept for joy. It was a strange meeting, for the brothers were sure that Joseph would hate them for the wicked thing they had done to him. Instead, he welcomed them with love and forgiveness. Now they were sure that God was with him.

WHAT DO YOU THINK?

What this story teaches: God wants His people to forgive others.

1. How would most people feel if someone sold them as a slave in a foreign country?
2. Why do you think Joseph's brothers were surprised when he forgave them and helped them? How would you have felt if you had been his brothers at that time?

A Ruff Day

"Where could he be?" Maxi moaned.

"This just isn't like Ruff to run away," said Mini. "I still think someone has dognapped him."

Ruff had been gone all day. Maxi and Mini had looked everywhere.

Maxi called all of his friends. But none of them had seen Ruff. At least, that's what they all said.

Mini called all of her friends. But none of them had seen Ruff either.

"Did you look in the playground at school?" Mini asked. "He might be waiting for us there."

"I looked there twice," said Maxi.

"How about Pookie's back yard?"

"I've been there twice also. And Maria's and Big Bill's and Charley's and everywhere else. He's GONE!"

Mini almost shivered when Maxi said "GONE." It sounded like Ruff was never coming back, and Mini couldn't think of Ruff never coming back.

"Mommi will be home from the grocery store soon," said Mini. "Perhaps she can drive us out to the woods. Maybe he went out there to chase squirrels."

"But he's never done that without us," Maxi argued.

When Mommi came home she drove Maxi and Mini to the woods to look for Ruff. They looked and looked, but Ruff was not there. At last they all went home, looking very sad.

"Poppi will be home in time for dinner," said Mommi. "He may have some ideas. I don't know where else to look."

Poppi listened carefully when Mini and Maxi told him all of the places they had gone. But Ruff was nowhere to be found.

"Please Poppi," they said. "Can't you think of some other place he may have gone?"

"I can't think of another place he could have gone," said Poppi. "But there is another place someone could have taken him."

"See! I told you he was dognapped," said Mini.

"He could have been picked up by the dogcatcher," said Poppi. "But the dogcatcher should have called us as soon as he saw Ruff's tag. Anyway, I don't know why he would pick Ruff up."

"Please, Poppi, let's go down there right now!" Maxi and Mini begged.

"Hmmm, it's too late tonight," said Poppi. "The dog pound won't be open until morning. But we will go down first thing."

Maxi and Mini didn't sleep very well that night. They both dreamed of dogs—little dogs, giant dogs, and dogs that had run away. Maxi dreamed about dogs that lived together in The Pound, a dog community where Ruff had gone to live. Mini dreamed about The Dognapper.

In the morning they fussed and fumed until it was time to go. All the way to the dog pound they kept asking Poppi why Ruff would be picked up.

"Yep! We have a little dog that fits the description," said the catcher. "Right this way."

Ruff yipped and yelped when he saw Maxi and Mini. Mini shed some tears and Maxi squeezed a couple out, too.

"Why did you pick him up?" Poppi asked.

"No tag," said the catcher. "This boy called and said he was a stray so we got him."

"BOY?" asked Maxi. "Who?"

"Hmmmm, here's the address," said the catcher.

"BIG BILL'S HOUSE!" Maxi shouted. "How could he do such a mean thing?"

"Looks like it's time to pay a visit to Bill's house," said Poppi.

Bill was very quiet when Poppi walked into the house with Bill's father. Bill didn't dare look at Maxi and Mini either.

"What can we do for you?" asked Bill's father.

When Poppi explained what had happened, Bill's father became very angry at Bill. "What the big idea?" he fumed. "Why did you take Ruff's tag off and turn him in?"

Big Bill shrunk down in his chair. Maxi had never seen him look so small before. Or so afraid.

"I . . . I was just trying to get even with Maxi for beating me in a game at school," he stammered.

"MAXI? That dog belongs to the whole family!" Bill's father stormed. "Now what if the Muffin Family tried to get even with you for this? What do you think THEY would do?"

Bill shrunk down in his chair even further. He wasn't sure what they would do. But it would be something quite bad.

Bill finally looked up at Poppi. He looked at Maxi and Mini. "I . . . I'm really sorry," he said. "That was a terrible thing to do. Please forgive me."

That night after dinner the Muffin Family read the story of Joseph forgiving his brothers. It reminded them of the time in Big Bill's living room that morning.

"I wanted to punch him in the nose!" said Maxi. "But I suppose Joseph wanted to punch his brothers in the nose many times."

"But you didn't!" said Poppi. "And neither did Joseph."

"I know," said Maxi. "I guess Jesus would have forgiven Bill if He had been there this morning."

"I guess He would have," said Poppi. "And that's why you did it, too."

LET'S TALK ABOUT THIS

What this story teaches: We should forgive others when they ask us.

1. How would you have felt if you had been Joseph and you could have had revenge on your mean brothers? How would you have felt if you had been Maxi and Bill had asked you to forgive him for his mean trick?
2. Why are we happier if we forgive? Why is it important for us to forgive others when we want God to forgive us?

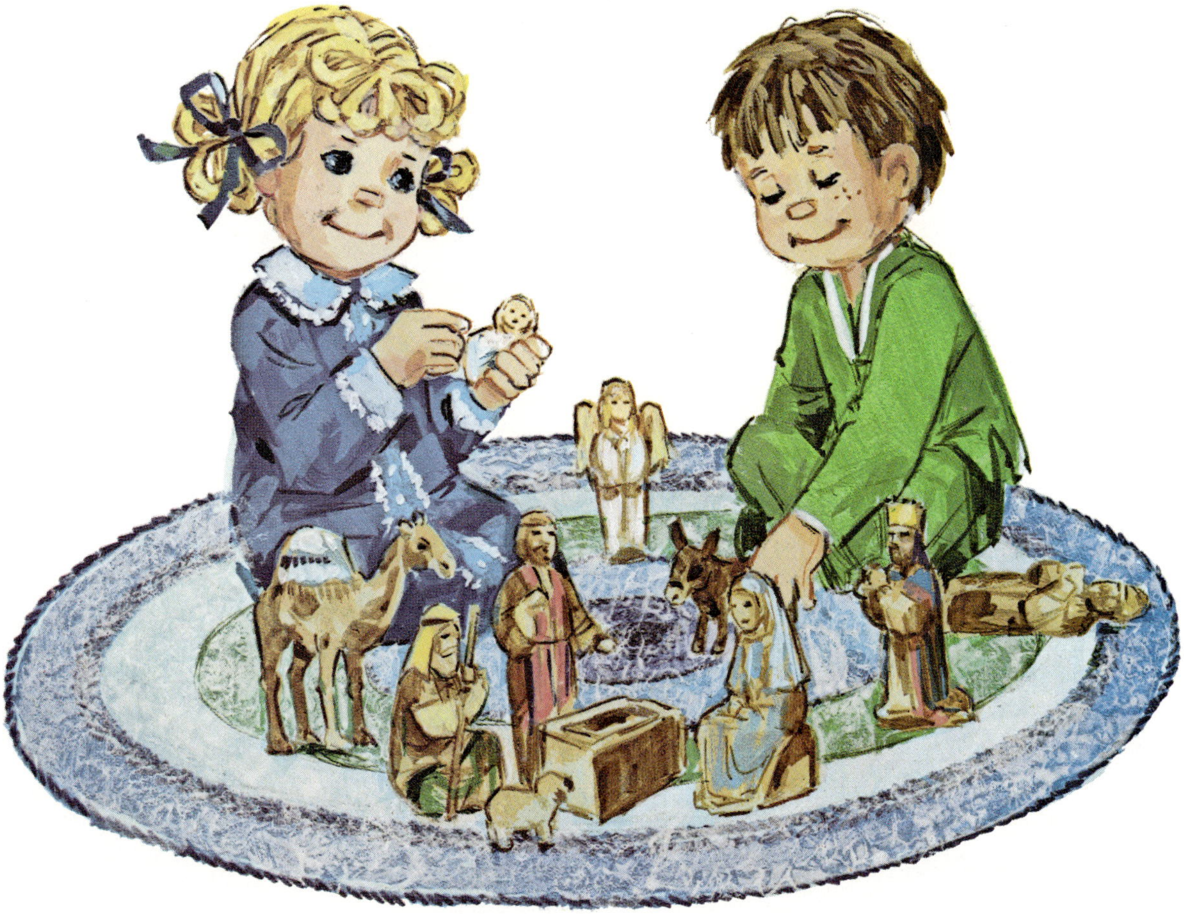

WHO IS THAT CHILD?

A Night That Changed the World

LUKE 2:1-20

"Those Romans!" Joseph grumbled as he came into his house. "They're always asking for something."

May looked up at her husband. It wasn't like Joseph to grumble. "Now what?" she asked softly.

"Taxes!" said Joseph. "We must all put our names on the Roman tax rolls. It's a decree from Caesar Augustus. We must go to Bethlehem to register, for that was the home of our ancestor David."

Mary smiled. "Then we will leave tomorrow," she said. "We can be there in three or four days."

"But you can't go!" said Joseph. "You're going to have a baby. It could come any day now."

"God will take care of the baby," Mary answered. "He will not let His Son be harmed."

Joseph thought for a moment. Mary was right. This was God's Son. Surely God would not let anything happen to Him.

So Mary and Joseph joined a caravan of travelers on their way to Jerusalem. From there, they would travel a few miles south to Bethlehem. People usually traveled together in caravans in those days to protect themselves from robbers.

It was a long, dusty trip, lasting several days. Mary probably rode on the family donkey as Joseph walked by her side. From Nazareth they went southward through the great plain, then up through the hills, covered with vineyards and olive groves.

Mary and Joseph were so tired by the time they reached Bethlehem. It was late in the afternoon, and they looked for an inn where they could stay.

"My wife and I would like a room in your inn," Joseph said to the innkeeper.

"So would everyone else!" said the innkeeper. "There isn't an empty room in Bethlehem. This tax decree has brought people from all over the land."

Joseph looked sad and frightened. "But my wife," he said, "is going to have a baby. Perhaps tonight! We must stay somewhere."

"You may sleep in the stable," said the innkeeper. "I have nothing else to give you."

"Then we will stay there," said Joseph.

Joseph looked sadly at Mary as they walked into the stable. "It isn't very good for you," he said softly. "What if the baby should come tonight?"

Mary smiled. "Then we will be glad we have a warm, dry stable for Him," she answered.

As the hours of the night passed by, the lights of the inn flickered and went out. Soon the guests were sound asleep. In the stable, the donkeys and camels closed their eyes and went to sleep, too.

And while Mary and Joseph were there, the Baby was born in the stable. Mary wrapped Him in wide strips of cloth and laid Him in the soft straw in a manger.

"We will name Him Jesus," said Mary, "just as the angel said we should."

As Mary and Joseph watched the Baby Jesus, they could not see the shepherds who were out on the hills near Bethlehem. It was cold on the hillsides, and the shepherds huddled near their fire.

But suddenly the shepherds looked up. "What's happening?" one of them whispered. "The sky is getting brighter and brighter. But it is a long time until morning."

Within a few moments, the shepherds could see the figure of an angel in the bright sky. They trembled with fear as the angel called out to them.

"You must not be afraid," the angel said. "I have good news for you. A Saviour was born tonight in Bethlehem. He will save His people from their sins, for He is God's Son, the Messiah."

The shepherds were still trembling as the angel continued. "You will find this Baby in a manger, wrapped in strips of cloth."

When the angel finished, a great number of angels appeared in the sky, praising God. It was like the sound of a mighty choir, filling the sky.

"Glory to God in the highest," the angels said. "Peace to all men on earth who please Him."

The sky dimmed, and the angels disappeared from sight. Soon the silence of the night was broken only by the movements of some sheep or the bleating of a lamb.

"Did it really happen?" asked one shepherd.

"Yes!" said the others. "We saw and heard it, too. Let's go to Bethlehem and see this wonderful thing that has happened."

The shepherds hurried across the lonely hills and through the deserted streets of Bethlehem. At last they found the stable. Softly they went in and found Mary and Joseph, watching over the newborn Baby.

"The Messiah!" whispered the shepherds.

"Then you know who He is," said Joseph.

"Yes, His birth was announced by the angels," the shepherds answered. Then they told of the great number of angels they had seen and heard.

Later, the shepherds returned to their sheep, their minds filled with the wonderful things they had seen and heard. And Mary and Joseph praised God for sending His Son, the promised Saviour.

WHAT DO YOU THINK?

What this story teaches: Jesus is God's Son, the Messiah.

1. Why was the birth of this Baby so special? Why do you think the angels announced it?
2. How do you know that Jesus is the Messiah, God's Son? Why is that important for you to know?

The New Pony for Tony Maloney

"Have you talked with Tony today?" Mini asked. "Is the new pony about to be born? Huh, Maxi?"

"Tony said it could be born tonight, or tomorrow, or any day now," Maxi answered. "I'm so anxious to see a new baby pony."

"Me, too!" said Mini. "That will be exiciting."

"Tony promised that he would call as soon as the pony is born," said Maxi. "Then we can go out to Tony's house to see it."

Every day that week Maxi asked Tony about the new pony. And every day that week Mini asked Maxi if he had asked Tony about the pony.

"Not yet," Tony answered. "But soon."

Maxi and Mini grew more excited as the days passed. Tony was excited, too. It wasn't every day that a new baby pony was born.

Early one Saturday morning the phone rang and Maxi answered. His face lit up like a lamp.

"Really? When? When can we come over? How's the mommi pony? What color is it?" and a dozen other questions rolled from Maxi.

Mini clapped her hands and jumped up and down. "It's here! It's here! Maxi, when can we go out to see the new baby pony?"

"NOW!" said Maxi.

Maxi and Mini asked Mommi if it was all right to go. Then they hurried to Tony's house at the edge of town. Tony was waiting for them in the pony barn.

"Oh, isn't that a darling little pony?" Mini cooed. "Isn't it just precious?"

"Yeah," Maxi said softly. "Wait until our friends hear about this."

"I've already called Bill and Maria and Charley," said Tony. "They're coming over this morning, too."

Maxi started to list some of the people he would call. And Mini named a dozen of her friends who would like to hear the good news.

What an exciting day this was for Maxi and Mini! By evening they had made at least three trips with different friends to see Tony's new baby pony. And they had each made at least a dozen phone calls about the pony.

When the Muffin Family sat down to eat dinner, Poppi asked Maxi to pray and thank God for the food. "And thank you for the new baby pony," Maxi prayed also.

"Amen!" said Mini.

"Have you two had a busy day?" Poppi asked.

Maxi told Poppi about the new pony, and Mini told

him how excited they were. Then Maxi told him how they had visited the new baby pony, and Mini told how they had each called their friends and went back with them to see the new pony.

"Well, that reminds me of the shepherds," said Poppi.

"What shepherds?" Mini asked.

"The shepherds who visited the Baby Jesus when He was born," said Poppi. "They were so excited when they left that they went everywhere, telling the Good News.

Poppi read about the shepherds in Luke 2: 17-18.

"Yeah! We were just like the shepherds," said Maxi.

"Except for one thing," said Poppi.

"What was that?" Mini asked.

"You and Maxi had good news to tell," said Poppi. "The shepherds had THE GOOD NEWS about Jesus' coming. It was news that was too good to keep. They just had to tell everyone."

"Is that why we still tell others about Jesus?" Maxi asked.

"Yes, it's still news that is too good to keep to ourselves," Poppi answered. "And when we're excited about Jesus, we will tell everyone we can about Him. Then they can accept Jesus into their lives, too."

"Wow! Just think what would happen if we all got as excited about the Good News as we did about the news of Tony's pony," said Maxi.

"Hmmm," said Poppi. "You've learned something very important from Tony's pony. Perhaps that pony will remind you to be like the shepherds."

LET'S TALK ABOUT THIS

What this story teaches: We should share the Good News about Jesus with others.

1. What is the most exciting news you have heard this year? Were you anxious to share it with your friends and family.

2. What is the difference between good news and the Good News? How can you share the Good News with others? Will you?

Rich Gifts for a New King

MATTHEW 2:1-12

In lands far to the east of Bethlehem, there lived some wise men. For many years they had studied the stars, waiting for a special star to appear. It would tell of the birth of a new King, a Great King above all other kings.

So when the star appeared one night, the wise men were excited. "The star!" they shouted. "It is here! The Great King has been born. We must go to find Him and take our precious gifts to Him."

The wise men hurried about, packing their gifts of gold, frankincense, and myrrh. They loaded their camels and rode toward the west where the star had appeared.

For many months they rode. At last they came to Jerusalem. Someone in Jerusalem would know about the great King, they were sure.

"We are searching for a great King who has been born," the wise men said. "Do you know about Him?"

But no one knew about the Great King. They knew only about King Herod, the evil king who ruled their land. Some of the people told King Herod about the wise men and the strange questions they asked about a Great King.

Of course, King Herod was disturbed about these questions. If there was a new king, he might some day take the kingdom from Herod. So King Herod called for the chief priests and wise men of his kingdom.

"What do you know about this Great King?" he demanded.

"He will be born in Bethlehem," they answered. "The prophet Micah wrote about this many years ago. He said that the Great King would rule Israel."

Herod was afraid when he heard this. He must not let it happen. Immediately he called for the wise men from the East and asked them about the star.

"Search for the Great King in Bethlehem," he said. "When you have found Him, tell me where He is so that I may go and worship Him also."

That night the star appeared to the wise men again as they rode toward Bethlehem. "The star!" they shouted. "It will lead us to the Great King."

So the wise men followed the star until it stood over

the house where Mary and Joseph lived with the Baby Jesus. There they brought forth their precious gifts for the Great King.

"My gift is gold," said one wise man. It was a gift for kings.

"And my gift is frankincense," said another. "It is the gift that speaks of holy living."

The third wise man presented his gift, too. "Myrrh is the gift of suffering," he said softly. "But it is a precious gift." Someday myrrh would be put on the body of Jesus when He was crucified.

That night the wise men had a dream. In their dream, God warned them not to return to Herod, for he wanted to kill the Baby Jesus. God told the men to go back to their homes some other way.

So the wise men left Bethlehem and made their way east to their own lands. But as they left, they turned once more to see the village of the Great King. How glad they were that they could bring their precious gifts to Him.

WHAT DO YOU THINK?

What this story teaches: Jesus wants our best gifts.

1. Why was King Herod afraid when he heard about the birth of a baby?
2. Why did the wise men travel so far to see this Child? Why did they bring such rich gifts to the Baby Jesus?

The Castle and the Pigpen

"Poppi."

"Yes, Maxi."

"Do you think people should give their BEST gifts to Jesus?"

"People who love Jesus should, Maxi."

"Should I give my best to Jesus?"

"Yes, Maxi."

"Why?"

"Because He gave His best for you."

"What was that, Poppi?"

"His life, Maxi."

"But if you give away your best, you have only the worst left for yourself."

"Maxi, let me tell you a parable about our best gifts. Then you can decide if that is true."

This is the parable Poppi told Maxi:

Once there were three great trees who lived together in the forest. One day a king came to one of the trees.

"Please give me wood to make my castle," the king asked. "But it must be your best wood, for only the best will do for a king's castle."

"Why should I give my best wood?" asked the tree. "I would have nothing left for myself. I am much too beautiful to become an ugly old castle."

So the tree sent down some leaves and sticks. The tree gave some of its rotten bark. But it would not give its best wood for the king's castle.

The king was sorry that the great tree had given such poor gifts. "I cannot build a beautiful castle with these gifts," he said. "I will ask another great tree."

So the king went to see the second great tree. "Please give me wood to build my castle," said the king. "But it must be your best wood, for only the best will do for a king's castle."

"Why should I give my best wood?" said the second great tree. "If I give my best wood, I must give myself. Then I would have nothing left for my own pleasure. I am much too beautiful to become an ugly old castle."

So the second great tree gave the king some nests which birds had built in its branches. It threw down fungus that had grown on its great trunk. But it would not give its best wood for the king's castle.

The king was sorry that the second tree had given no better gifts than the first. "I cannot build a beautiful castle with these," he said. "I will ask the third great tree for the wood."

The king went to the third great tree, not far from the first two. "Please give me wood to build my castle," said the king. "But it must be your best wood, for only the best will do for a king's castle."

The great tree sighed. It sounded like wind blowing through its branches. "To give you my best, I must give you myself," said the great tree. "But I will give you all I have, for only the best will do for a king's beautiful castle."

Woodsmen came and cut down the third great tree while the other two watched with scorn. "Foolish tree!" they said as it crashed to the forest floor. "You are giving yourself away. But we will keep ourselves towering in the forest. We will not give ourselves for any king."

The two selfish trees watched each day as the king's men built the beautiful castle. The great tree that gave himself was cut and polished and fitted together until even the king clapped his hands with joy.

Each day after the great tree had become a king's castle, he told his two fellow trees of all the beautiful things he enjoyed. Kings from faraway lands dined in his banquet hall and talked about his beauty. Lovely ladies sang songs to the king about the tree that had given himself away to become the king's home. And princes and princesses played and laughed within his walls.

The two selfish trees began to grow jealous. As they did, their leaves withered, and they became ugly, not like the proud, beautiful trees they once were.

One day the king gave orders to his royal carpenters. "I must have some pens for my pigs," he said. "Cut down the two ugliest trees of the forest and make the pigpens from them."

So the royal carpenters cut down the two selfish trees and made the royal pigpens from them. There was great squealing and oinking when the pigs went to live in their new pens.

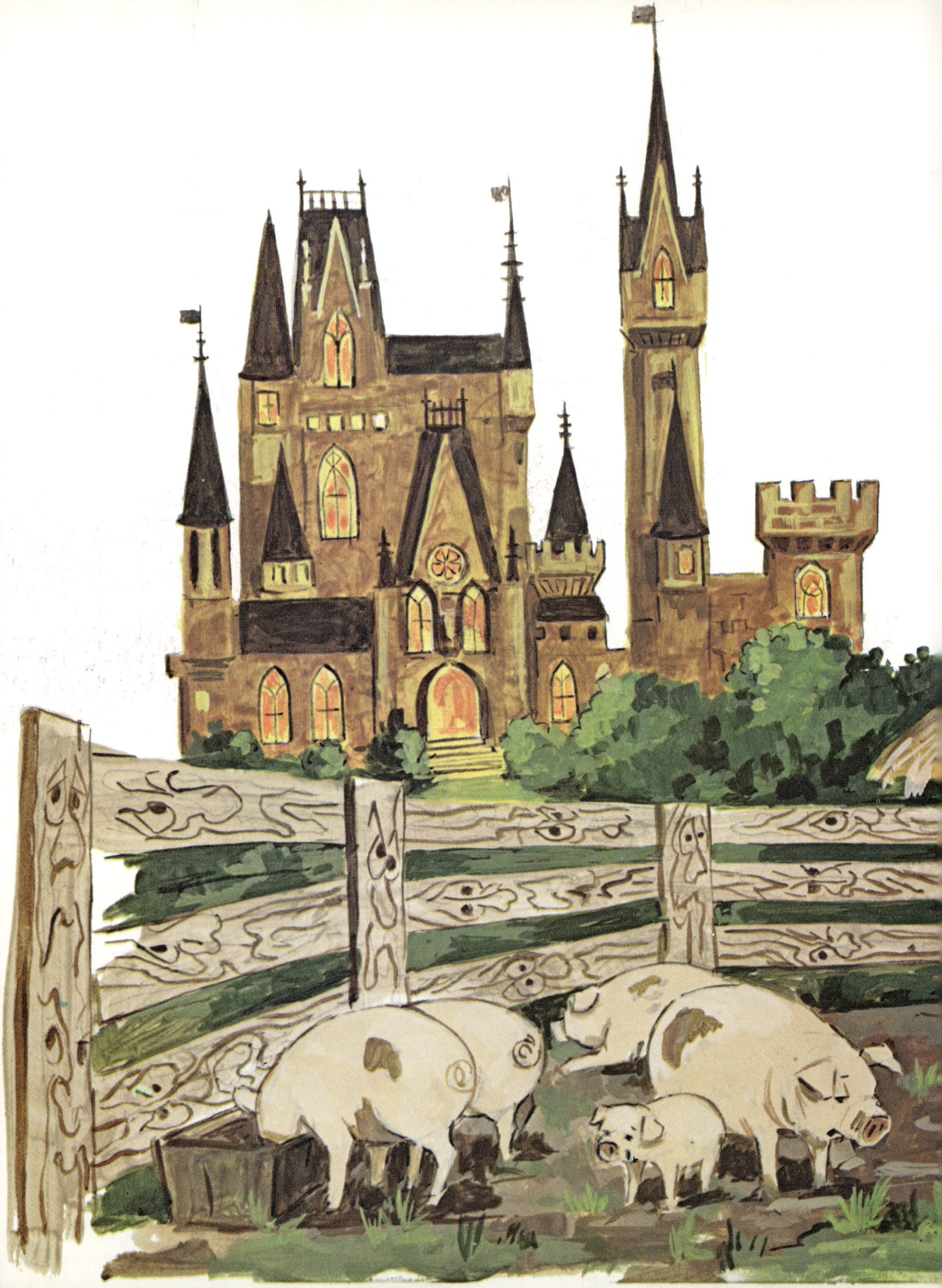

Each day the great tree that gave himself to become a castle sang songs about the music and laughter and banquets which went on within his walls. The songs were easily heard in the pigpens. But the two selfish trees which gave only bark and sticks and fungus could not sing. They could only complain about the oinks and squeals and smells of pigs.

When Poppi finished the parable of the castle and the pigpen he waited for Maxi to say something.

"Does that mean that Jesus wants to chop me up and make something different out of me?" Maxi asked.

"Not unless you're a tree," said Poppi. "You can give your best to Jesus in other ways."

"Like what?" asked Maxi.

"Like using your best talents for Jesus," said Poppi. "Or reading your Bible and praying during the best part of your day. Or perhaps giving money for Jesus' work that you would rather spend on yourself. I'm sure you can think of other ways to give YOUR best to Jesus."

That night Maxi prayed, "Lord, help me give my best to you so I can be like the king's castle. Help me not to keep my best for myself and become like a pigpen. Amen."

Poppi smiled when he heard Maxi pray. But he whispered softly, "Lord, let that be my prayer, too. Amen."

LET'S TALK ABOUT THIS

What this story teaches: We should give Jesus our best.

1. What are some ways you can give your best for Jesus? Are you giving Him your best now? Would you like to?
2. Why not make a little sign to put on your wall? It might read something like this: TODAY I WILL GIVE MY BEST FOR JESUS. Then try each day to give Him something that is your best.
3. Look up these Bible verses about Jesus giving Himself away and talk about them: John 12: 23-26.

The Journey to Egypt
MATTHEW 2:13-23; LUKE 2:39

Word soon reached King Herod that the wise men were gone. They would not return to tell him where he could find the Child whose star had led them from the east.

Herod was furious when he heard about this. No one dared to trick him! He would kill the wise men if he could find them. But of course they were far away from Herod's kingdom, so there was nothing he could do to them.

As Herod thought about these things, he grew angry and afraid. Somewhere in Bethlehem there was a Child who would become a great king. Herod was sure that this Child could take his kingdom from him. He must never let that happen.

"I want him killed!" Herod told his soldiers. "Now!"

"But who is he?" they asked. "There are many young boys in Bethlehem. Which one do we kill?"

"How do I know?" Herod bellowed. "Kill them all!"

The soldiers ran from Herod's palace. They knew they must kill the Child or Herod would kill them. So they left immediately for Bethlehem.

While all of this was happening, an angel appeared to Joseph as he was sleeping. The angel brought a warning to Joseph.

"You must leave for Egypt tonight," the angel said. "King Herod wants to kill the Child Jesus. Hurry! Take Mary and the Child and stay in Egypt until I tell you that it is safe to come home."

Joseph woke Mary, and they quickly packed the few things they owned into some bags. Before long they made their way quietly through the streets and out into the countryside. By morning they were far from Bethlehem, where Herod's soldiers killed every baby boy under two years old.

It was many days before Joseph and Mary reached Egypt with the Child Jesus. "This will be our home until the angel tells us to return to our own land," they said.

Day by day Mary and Joseph watched the Child grow. The Child learned many things during the months the family stayed in Egypt. Mary and Joseph taught Him about their people back home. And they taught Him about God.

One night after King Herod had died, Joseph had a dream. Through his dream God spoke to him and told him that it was now time to return home with Mary and Jesus.

It was exciting to pack for the trip home. And it was even more exciting to head toward home again.

Joseph asked each traveler he met about the things that had happened in their land. He was anxious to hear how King Herod had died and who would take his place.

But Joseph was sorry to hear that Herod's son was already the new king. He was as wicked as King Herod. Perhaps more wicked.

Joseph wondered then if he should return to Bethlehem. Would Jesus ever be safe there again?

That night God spoke to Joseph through another dream. "Return to your hometown of Nazareth," God said to Joseph. "Do not go to live in Bethlehem."

It took many days to travel to Nazareth. But Mary and Joseph were so happy to be back. Before long, Joseph set up his carpenter's shop and no doubt taught the Boy Jesus to make many things from wood.

As the years passed, Jesus grew strong and tall. He

grew wiser, too, and people began to see that He was more than a young carpenter. Some wondered how He knew so much about God. But Mary and Joseph knew, for God had chosen them to take care of His Son.

WHAT DO YOU THINK?

What this story teaches: God wants fathers and mothers to take care of their family, just as He takes care of them.

1. Why did Mary and Joseph take the Boy Jesus to live in Egypt? What caused them to return home to Nazareth?
2. In what way was Jesus more than just another boy? Who was He?

Take Care of Your Family

"Are you coming with me, Mini?"

"Sure, Maxi. Did you ask Mommi if it's OK for us to go to Tony's house?"

"Yeah. She said it's fine as long as we're back in time for dinner."

Ever since Tony's pony's baby pony had been born, Maxi and Mini went often to Tony's house to see it. They liked to go especially when Tony fed his pony.

Tony had told Maxi when to come so they could watch the mother pony eat. "In fact, I'll even let you help me feed her," he said.

Tony scooped up some feed in a pail and gave it to Maxi. "Put it in the feedbox," he said. "Then we'll get the mother pony and her baby in here."

Tony's pony didn't need to be asked a second time! She ran into the stable with the baby pony at her side.

"Wow! Look at her eat that feed!" said Maxi.

"And look at the baby pony," said Mini. "He's going to eat his lunch, too."

The baby pony came to the mother and began to drink milk from her. The mother seemed perfectly happy for the baby pony to get his lunch as long as she could have hers.

"That's neat!" said Maxi. "You take care of your pony. Then she takes care of her baby."

"Just like a people family," said Mini.

"How's that, Mini?" asked Tony.

"Well, Mommi and Poppi take care of Maxi and me," she said. "Then we take care of Ruff and Tuff and feed them."

Maxi and Mini sat with Tony on some bales of straw and talked about this. At last the mother pony finished eating and so did her baby. Then they both ran outside.

"She's a little messy," said Mini. "Look how much she spilled on the ground.

"If we're quiet," said Tony, "another family will eat that."

So the three of them waited quietly and watched the feed that the mother pony had spilled. Suddenly a mother duck came by and saw the feed. She ran toward it, quacking noisily. Five little ducklings waddled through the stable doorway and began to share in the feed.

"Did you see how the mother duck called her little ducklings?" Mini asked. "When she quacked, they knew that she had found some food."

"Yeah, look at them eat," Maxi added. "Your pony's garbage is their feast."

Before long the ducks had finished their meal and

ran happily out of the doorway. The three friends sat quietly on the bales of straw to see what would happen next.

"If we're quiet," Tony whispered, "you may see another family come by."

In a few minutes a mother mouse scurried from a little hole beneath the feedbox. The three friends stopped whispering.

The mother mouse looked around carefully. Then she scurried back into the hole and returned with three little mice.

Mini wanted to squeal with delight and talk about the "cute little mice," but Tony shushed her with his finger at his lips. The mother mouse and her little ones ate loose grains of feed that the mother duck and her ducklings had missed. At last they were filled, and they ran back into the mouse hole to take a nap.

"They were so DARR-ling!" Mini cooed.

"You ought to set some traps and catch those

mice," said Maxi, talking a little like he knew what he was talking about.

"MAX-I!!!" Mini shouted. "Don't you say such things. Who would want to kill those darling little things?"

"Oh, nobody. Nobody at all," said Maxi. "Maybe we could catch them and put them in your bed."

With that, Maxi reached out his fingers and ran them up Mini's back. Mini let out a little screech and then laughed with Maxi about it.

"Thanks, Tony," Maxi said. "Now Mini and I have to go home."

"What for?" asked Tony.

"So Mommi and Poppi can share their food with us," said Maxi.

"He means it's almost dinner time," Mini explained. "But who shares food with Mommi and Poppi?" Mini added on the way home.

"God does!" said Maxi.

And that gave Mini something to think about all the way home.

LET'S TALK ABOUT THIS

What this story teaches: We should thank God and our parents for taking care of us.

1. How did Joseph take care of Mary and the Baby Jesus in the Bible story, "A Journey to Egypt?"
2. How did each animal in this story help to take care of its family? How did Mommi and Poppi take care of their family? Who takes care of you? Do you ever thank your parents for taking care of you? Do you ever thank God for taking care of your parents and you? Why not do that now?

105

A Visit to God's House

LUKE 2:41-50

There was excitement in the air as young Jesus and Mary and Joseph joined the caravan leaving Nazareth for Jerusalem. Aunts, uncles, cousins, and friends were all headed for the great Passover Feast.

Each man and boy had to go to this feast, which took place every spring. But it was such an exciting time that most of the men took their entire families. Jerusalem hummed with activity as friends met to talk and worship together in the Temple.

This was a special year for young Jesus, for He was now twelve and was thought of as a man. That meant He could do many more things in Jerusalem than before. His family would not be asking "Where's Jesus?" all the time, for He would be joining in the groups of men who sat to talk, instead of playing with the children.

There was shouting and singing as the caravan set forth, passing through the broad plain first, then heading through the hills toward the great city. Spring had carpeted the hills with wild flowers, and the groves of olive trees sighed in the soft spring breeze. It was truly a wonderful time to travel to Jerusalem.

Toward the end of the third day, the caravan began to climb the winding paths that led up to the city. There was shouting and singing as the people approached the great gates that led into Jerusalem.

The city was filled with many sounds. Donkeys

clopped along on the stone pavement, stopping now and then to give their long brays that echoed through the streets. The crowds chattered noisily by the hundreds of booths made of branches and leaves. The people stayed in these booths while they were in the city.

During the days of the feast, Jesus went about through the city, meeting friends and relatives, visiting the Temple, and doing things that any twelve-year-old boy would want to do. At last the time began when people took down their booths and prepared to head home.

Mary and Joseph gathered with their neighbors and

friends from Nazareth and formed the caravan. "Where is Jesus?" Mary asked Joseph, as they joined the caravan.

Joseph probably shrugged his shoulders. "Where has He been since we came to Jerusalem?" he may have said with a smile. "He must be with the other young men in the caravan. He is twelve now, you know, and we must not ask where He is every moment."

But Mary looked worried as they headed northward toward Nazareth. Throughout the day, she kept looking about to see if she could catch some sight of Jesus.

When the caravan stopped for the night and the people sat around their campfires to talk, Jesus had still not come back. Mary was quite worried by now.

"I haven't seen Jesus all day," she told Joseph. "I'm worried about Him."

Joseph nodded. "I will ask our friends and neighbors if they have seen Him," he whispered.

Much later Joseph returned, looking worried himself by now. "I'm afraid He isn't with our caravan," he said to Mary. "We must go back to Jerusalem to find Him."

The next morning the caravan went on toward Nazareth. But Mary and Joseph returned to Jerusalem alone. For three days they looked in all the familiar places their family had visited, but could not find Jesus. At last they came to the Temple.

"He loves God's house," said Joseph. "Perhaps He is still here. We will ask the teachers if they have seen Him."

When Mary and Joseph came into the room where the teachers sat, they were so surprised. There was Jesus, sitting among the teachers, talking with them about God. The teachers were surprised, too, for Jesus knew more about God's Word than some of them did.

"We have been looking for You for three days," said Mary. "Why have you done this to us?"

"But I have been here all the time," said Jesus. "I have been doing something important for my Father in heaven."

Mary and Joseph did not know what to say. They knew that God was Jesus' Father. But the teachers did not know.

Later, Mary and Joseph and Jesus made their way back to Nazareth. Mary and Joseph thought often about the things they had seen and heard. And Jesus continued to grow taller and wiser, pleasing God and others in all that He did.

WHAT DO YOU THINK?

What this story teaches: God wants us to love His house as Jesus did.

1. What does this story tell you about the Passover Feast? What does it tell you about Jesus' family?
2. How could Jesus know enough about God to talk with the wisest teachers? Where did He learn about God?

109

The "What If" Game

"Poppi, we had so much fun in Sunday school this morning," said Maxi. "I'm glad we go to our church."

"So am I," said Poppi. "But do you know why you're glad?"

Maxi looked puzzled. "Well, I'm just glad, I guess. I suppose I like everything."

"Let's have a little fun this afternoon, Maxi," said Poppi. "We'll go to our church and play a 'what if' game."

Maxi had never heard of a "what if" game before, but he thought it would be fun as long as he could play it with Poppi.

After dinner Poppi and Maxi walked back to their church. As they did, they talked about the time Jesus visited the temple in Jerusalem and how Jesus loved God's house.

At last Poppi and Maxi reached their church. But they didn't go inside yet.

"Maxi, we'll start the 'what if' game outside. We're going to pretend that certain things are suddenly taken away. OK, let's start with the steeple. What if the steeple blew down and we never put it back again?"

"I would miss it," said Maxi. "I like our steeple. It looks like it reaches up toward God."

"I like it, too," said Poppi. "But would this still be God's house if the steeple was gone?"

"Yes, it would," said Maxi. "But I still like it."

Poppi and Maxi walked inside. They went to Maxi's Sunday school room.

"Hmmm, what if we dumped out all these tables and chairs?" Poppi asked.

"You can't do that!" Maxi said, almost angrily. "We have fun sitting in our chairs and working in our books on the tables."

"You like them?"

110

"Of course!"

"But if they were all gone, would this still be God's house?"

"Yes, but I still like our chairs and tables. They help to make God's house fun."

"What about all those pictures and song books and lesson books, Maxi. What if we put all those in the garbage?"

"No! I wouldn't let you! I like to look at those pictures while I listen to our teacher. And we have fun singing from the song books and doing our work in the lesson books."

"But if we threw all these things away, would this still be God's house?"

"Yes, it would, but I still like all of these things. And so do my friends. These things all help to make God's house fun."

Maxi and Poppi went upstairs. They walked quietly into the large room where the church services were held.

"Couldn't we sell that piano and organ?" Poppi said. "Think of the money we could get for them. What if those were gone?"

"But they help us have beautiful music in our services," said Maxi. "We need them."

"Hmmm," said Poppi. "What about the place for the choir? And what about the choir itself? What if those were taken away?"

"I love to listen to the choir," said Maxi. "Especially when Mommi sings in it. It just wouldn't be the same here without our choir."

"But what if we sold our piano and organ and stopped having choir?" Poppi asked. "Would this still be God's house?"

"Yes, it would," Maxi answered. "But I still like the piano and organ and choir. They all help to make God's house fun."

Poppi looked around. He pointed to the pulpit.

"What if we took the pulpit out and told our preacher to get a job somewhere else?"

Maxi looked almost shocked. "Poppi! How could you say such a thing?"

"Just asking 'What if,'" said Poppi. "Apparently you wouldn't like that?"

"No!" said Maxi. "This church just wouldn't be the same without a pastor."

"But would it still be God's house?" Poppi asked.

Maxi thought for a moment. "I guess it would, but I still want our pastor here. He helps to make God's house fun, too."

Poppi looked at all of the pews where the people sat during the services. "You know, we could clear those out of here and have a lot more room for something. What if we did that?"

"Poppi! That's where we sit for the services!" Maxi was almost arguing by this time.

"But it would still be God's house, wouldn't it?"

"Yes, but I like to sit in the pews. If we had no place to sit the people might stay home."

"Would this still be God's house if they did?" Poppi asked.

Maxi thought for a long time. "Probably. Depends on what we did here."

"Well, what if we came to this building each Sunday to attend a big carnival?" said Poppi. "Would this still be God's house?"

"I . . . I guess not," said Maxi.

"But what if all the same people came," said Poppi.

"And what if we kept all the song books in the corner and the piano and organ where it is. And what if we kept all the pews, but moved them to the walls and had our carnival?"

"It's just not the same!" said Maxi. "I wouldn't think of it as God's house then."

"Then you know now, Maxi, what you like best of all here, don't you?" said Poppi. "This is God's house because it is a place where we come with God's people to learn about God and worship Him. We come here to sing about Him and praise Him. And we come to Sunday school to learn His Word and how we should put it to work in our lives."

"But I still like all those things you talked about in the 'what if' game," said Maxi.

"Of course you do," said Poppi. "Because they all help you to learn more about God and worship Him better. And that's why God's people have put them here."

"I'm glad this is our church," said Maxi. "And because we came here to play the 'what if' game this afternoon, I'm more glad than ever."

LET'S TALK ABOUT THIS

What this story teaches: We should love God's house and do all we can to take care of it.

1. What did you learn about your church from this story? Would you be happy if your church was torn down and all the people moved away?
2. What can you do to help others enjoy your church more? How about thanking God for His house now?

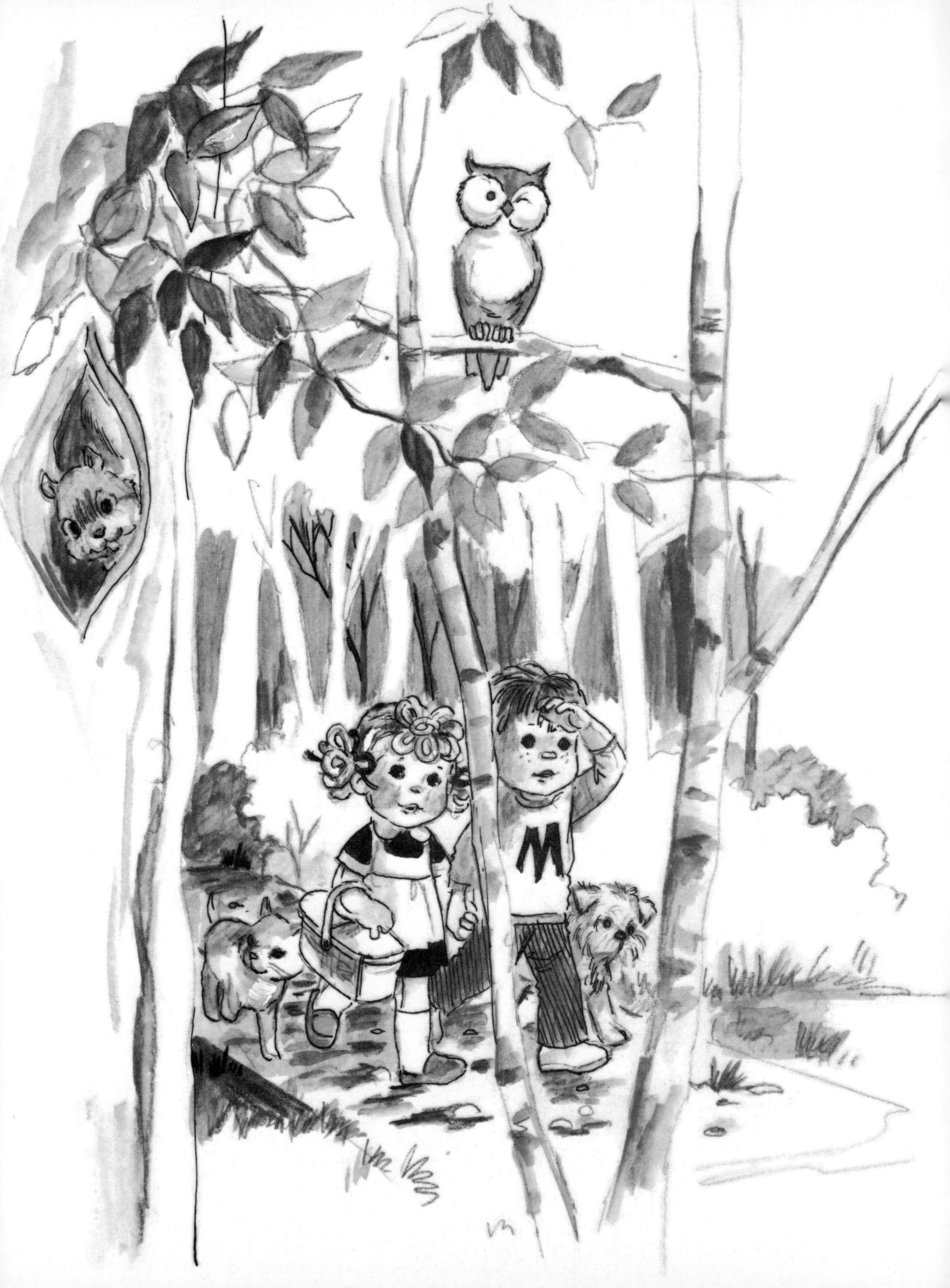

MARCHING THROUGH STRANGE PLACES

Food from Heaven

EXODUS 15:1, 22—16:36

The people of Israel were so happy to be free from their slavery in Egypt. As they watched God send the Red Sea over their masters, they sang and praised Him.

There would be no more bricks to make. No more Egyptian taskmasters forcing them to work for the king. They were free! And they were happy.

The caravan turned toward the wilderness and began to move forward. But the wilderness was a harsh place. There was no water. And there was no food.

As the days passed, the people became nervous and afraid. By the end of the third day, many of them were grumbling.

"Our water is almost gone," some said.

"So is ours," said others.

There was nothing in sight, either, except the rocks and sand and dust. There were no beautiful trees where they could find shade, and only a few scraggly bushes for the sheep and goats to eat.

Children began to cry. Mothers and fathers grumbled and complained even more.

"Do you want us to die of thirst?" they shouted angrily at Moses.

At last it seemed that the people could not take another step. Suddenly someone saw a lovely oasis ahead.

"Water!" the people shouted. Everyone was so excited. The mothers and fathers and children all ran to the water to drink.

But when they took their first gulp of water, they spit it out. "It's bitter!" they cried out. "Now what do we do?"

Then God showed Moses a tree. "Cut down the tree and throw it into the water," God told Moses. When this was done, the water was no longer bitter. The people drank until they were filled.

Not long after that, the people came to another oasis called Elim. It was a beautiful place with twelve springs and seventy palm trees. So the people camped beside the springs and rested for several days.

But there was still no food to be found in the wilderness. It would not be long now until all the food they had brought from Egypt would be gone.

"What will we do then?" some wondered. "Where will we find food in this place?"

Day by day the people grumbled and complained more. Many began to say mean things to Moses again.

"If you had only left us back in Egypt," they said, "we would have plenty to eat."

The people often talked of the melons and fish they had back home. There had been vegetables and fruits, too. But not here! The more they dreamed of the foods they had eaten in Egypt, the more they hated Moses and the wilderness.

One day the Lord spoke to Moses. "I'm going to rain food down from heaven," He said. "The people will have all the food they can eat. This evening they will have meat. In the morning they will have bread."

When Moses told the people about that, they could hardly believe it. Food? Here in the wilderness? Raining down from heaven? How could it be?

That evening God sent great flocks of quail to the camp. The birds flew so low that the people easily caught all they could eat.

The next morning the people awoke and looked outside their tents. "What's that on the ground?" they asked.

"It is the bread God promised to send," said Moses.

Covering the ground were thousands of white flakes, which became known as manna. "Pick up enough for today," Moses warned. "Do not take any more. You must trust God to send manna again tomorrow."

Of course some of the people wanted to do things their own way. "Who cares what Moses says?" they argued. "When everyone else is hungry, we'll have food to eat. What if God doesn't send manna tomorrow?"

But the next day their manna smelled rotten. It was filled with worms. Now the people knew that they must take only enough for the day. They must trust God to send the manna again the next day.

On the seventh day, the Sabbath, the Lord did not

118

send manna. It was a day of rest. But the people had been told to pick up enough the day before to feed them on the Sabbath. When they obeyed God, their manna did not spoil.

Each day God gave them enough to eat. But the next day they had to trust Him to send more. It was an important lesson for the people to learn.

WHAT DO YOU THINK?

What this story teaches: God gives us our food.

1. Why do you think God let the people get thirsty and hungry before He gave them food and water? Why didn't He give it to them as soon as they left Egypt?
2. What lesson did you learn from the manna? Why is this important for you to know?

Eggs

"Are we having eggs for breakfast?" Mini asked. "I don't like eggs. They're yukky."

Mommi had just taken some eggs from the refrigerator. She was ready to make one of her delicious omelets.

"Eggs are good food," said Mommi. "God gave them to us. Unless you're allergic to them you should enjoy them."

"What is allergic?" Mini asked.

"Allergic means that a certain food causes your body to itch, or that you can't breath well when you eat it," Mommi answered.

"I still don't like eggs, even though I'm not allergic to them," said Mini. "I wish God hadn't made eggs, then I wouldn't have to eat the yukky things."

"All right, Mini," said Mommi. "Let's make a deal. I promise that I will not give you eggs all week if you promise not to eat any eggs and not to complain."

"I promise," said Mini.

"NO eggs," said Mommi as she put the eggs back into the refrigerator. "Now what would you like for breakfast?"

"Pancakes!" said Mini. "I love them."

"Sorry, but pancakes are made with eggs," said Mommi. "You can't have pancakes. You promised that you would have NO eggs and that you would NOT complain."

Mini almost pouted. But she tried not to.

"OK, I'll have french toast," said Mini. "That's my second favorite."

"No french toast," said Mommi. "That's made with eggs, too."

"Waffles?" Mini asked softly, afraid that Mommi would say no again.

"Eggs, too!" said Mommi. "But keep trying."

"Well, how about some hot chocolate and a donut?" said Mini.

"You can have the hot chocolate, but you'll have to give up your marshmallow," said Mommi. "There are eggs in marshmallows. And NO donuts."

Mini did pout a little now as she drank her hot chocolate without a marshmallow and ate a bowl of cereal. She didn't say any more about eggs until the middle of the morning when she came running in with Maxi.

"Guess what?" she said. "Maxi just earned some money mowing a lawn. He said he would treat me to a chocolate sundae at Pop's Sweet Shop. May we go, Mommi, please?"

"Maxi may go," said Mommi. "But you promised that there would be no eggs this week."

"But Mommi, I don't want eggs, I want a chocolate sundae!" Mini whined.

"But Mini, there are eggs in ice cream, and you must have ice cream for the chocolate sundae. Sorry!" Mommi answered. "I guess you'll have to go by yourself, Maxi."

Mini almost cried when Maxi went down the sidewalk toward town. "Well, could I go with him and have some chocolate meringue pie?" Mini asked.

"No, there are eggs in meringue and in the pie crust," said Mommi.

"Then I'll just go have a candy bar in our kitchen," Mini mumbled, trying not to complain.

Mommi looked at the candy bar. "This is a filled bar," said Mommi. "You can't have it. It has eggs in it."

"Cake?" asked Mini.

"Sorry," said Mommi. "Cake has eggs."

"Cookies?"

"No."

"Then how about some root beer?"

"Sorry, that has eggs, too."

"MOMMI!" Mini almost screamed. "Then how about a muffin? Please can't a Mini Muffin have a muffin?"

"No! That has eggs, too, Mini."

Mini sat in the corner of the dinette and looked very sad. But when Mommi saw her she reminded Mini of their bargain.

"Remember! You were the one who said no eggs," said Mommi. "And you promised not to complain."

"I'm not complaining," said Mini. "I'm just thinking."

"What are you thinking, Mini?" Mommi asked.

"I'm just thinking how much I DO like eggs," said Mini. "I'm just thinking how many good things God had in mind when He made eggs."

"Mini."

"Yes, Mommi."

"You could still catch up to Maxi if you hurry."

"Oh, Mommi! Could we stop this silly thing about eggs?"

"Of course, Mini. Have a good time at Pop's Sweet Shop!"

"This is EGGSCITING!" Mini shouted as she ran through the door. Then Mini stopped.

"Mommi," she called back. "Can we have eggs for breakfast tomorrow morning?"

"EGGSACTLY!" said Mommi.

LET'S TALK ABOUT THIS

What this story teaches: We should thank God for giving us good food to eat.

1. What did Mini learn about eggs?
2. Are there some foods you don't like? Do you complain about them? What will you do about them now?
3. Who gives us our foods? Who gave the manna to the people of Israel in the wilderness? Do you thank God for your food each time you eat? Will you? And will you appreciate each food, even the ones you may think you don't like?

With God on a Mountain

EXODUS 19—20

Day after day the people of Israel walked through the wilderness. They formed a great caravan, with mothers and fathers, boys and girls, flocks and herds, and all that the people had brought from their homes in Egypt.

After three months, the people arrived in the land surrounding Mount Sinai. Moses had been a shepherd in this land when God spoke to him from a burning bush. Now God had sent Moses back to Egypt to free his people from their slavery.

While the people stayed in camp, Moses climbed to the top of the mountain. God met Moses there and spoke to him.

"Tell the people of Israel to obey Me," God said. "If they do, I will go with them and help them, and they will be My special people."

When Moses returned to camp, he told the leaders of the people what God had said. "We will obey Him," they promised. "We will do all that He asks."

Moses made another trip into the mountain to talk with God. He told God how the people had promised to obey Him.

Then God arranged for a special meeting with Moses. It would be a meeting the people would never forget.

"I will come to you in a dark cloud," God said to Moses. "The people will hear Me speak, and they will know that I have talked with you. Tell the people to wash their clothes and be ready to hear Me, for I will come in three days."

God warned that the people must not come on the mountain. Anyone who did would be put to death.

The people did exactly as God had said. They washed their clothes and waited for the third day to come.

On the morning of the third day, the mountain shook with thunder and lightning. Thick, dark clouds came down upon it.

"Listen!" the people cried out. They began to tremble as the sound of a great trumpet rang out across the camp.

Moses led the people to the foot of Mount Sinai, as God had said he should. The people were afraid as they watched smoke billow up from the mountain into the sky. It was like the smoke of a great furnace.

When Moses spoke to God, He answered in a voice like thunder. Then God told Moses to come up into the mountain again.

When Moses returned to the top of Mount Sinai, he brought Aaron with him. There God gave ten special rules for the people to obey.

1. Never worship any gods but Me.
2. Never make gods, idols, or images looking like animals, birds, or fish to bow down to or worship. Give Me all your love.
3. Never swear or use My name in a foolish way.
4. Honor the Sabbath day. Make the Sabbath a holy day, a day of rest.
5. Honor your father and mother.
6. Never kill a person.
7. Never love someone else's husband or wife.
8. Never steal.
9. Never lie.
10. Never want what belongs to others.

By the time Moses and Aaron returned from the mountain, the people were shaking with fear. They were afraid that God would kill them.

"You must not be afraid," Moses said to the people. "God is giving these rules so that you may please Him. When you please Him, it will make you happy, for you will not want to sin against Him."

"Then we will please Him in all that we do," the people promised, "for we want to be happy, too."

WHAT DO YOU THINK?

What this story teaches: God wants us to obey His rules, for that pleases Him.

1. Why do you think God gave His people rules? Why can't people do what they please? Would that make them happy?
2. Why should people want to obey God and please Him? Wouldn't it be more fun to please themselves?

Rules

"Maxi, will you please not put your feet on the sofa while your shoes are on?" Poppi asked. "You know the rules about that."

Maxi mumbled a little "umff" and put his feet down. Then he scrunched down and kept reading his book.

Maxi had read about five lines when Mommi walked into the living room. "Maxi, you must put a coaster under your glass of pop," she said. "You know how a wet glass leaves a ring on our wood table. That's the rule, you know."

Maxi mumbled another little "umff" and went to get a coaster to put under his glass. Then he settled down to read.

After he read about five lines Maxi put his book down. "Rules!" he grumbled. "Why do we have to have rules? If I were a Mommi or Poppi I'd throw out all the rules and let my kids do what they thought was best. Poppi, wouldn't we all be happier without rules?" Maxi asked.

"No, Maxi," said Poppi. "Rules help to make us happy."

"But why?" Maxi asked.

"Because rules keep us from doing things that hurt others," said Poppi. "Sometimes they keep us from hurting God."

Maxi kicked off his shoes and lay back on the sofa to think about that. He was sure that he would be happier if he did not have rules to bug him.

Before long Maxi fell fast asleep. And guess what he dreamed about? Rules!

In his dream Maxi was driving a little green car. He was so excited for he had always wanted to drive. This was a special car for it was new and was the kind that looked neat. And Mini was riding in the front with him.

Maxi dreamed that they were coming to the corner at Main Street downtown. "You'd better slow down," Mini warned. "There's a stoplight ahead."

"Why?" Maxi asked. "It's green."

But just as Maxi got to Main Street a big red car came roaring across and smashed into Maxi's cute little green car. Then the big red car began to drive away and leave Maxi's green car a crumpled mess.

"Look who's driving!" said Mini. "It's Big Bill!"

"You dumb guy," Maxi shouted. "I had the green light."

"Who cares," said Bill. "There are no more rules." Then he drove away, laughing at Maxi and his crumpled green car.

128

Suddenly Maxi's dream changed, and he was pulling his wrecked green car home on the sidewalk. As they came near their house, Ruff ran out to meet them. But as Ruff came toward them, the dogcatcher roared up in his truck and snatched Ruff and began to drive away. Maxi saw that the dogcatcher was Big Bill.

"Stop!" Maxi shouted. "What are you doing?"

"Taking him to the dog pound!" Bill shouted back.

"But you can't do that! He hasn't done anything wrong," said Maxi.

"Who cares?" said Bill. "There are no more rules."

Maxi was almost crying when he got home. He dropped his wrecked green car on the front lawn and ran up to his room. He wanted to shut the door and be alone. Yet who should be sitting in his room with his shoes up on Maxi's bed but Big Bill.

"You get out of here or I'll call the police," Maxi shouted.

Big Bill grinned. "YOU get out kid," he shouted. "This is my room now. There are no police. Remember? There are NO MORE RULES."

Maxi ran down the stairs to find Poppi. "POPPI! POPPI!" he shouted.

"What is it, Maxi?" Poppi answered. "Are you having a bad dream?"

Maxi blinked his eyes. He was lying on the sofa in his own living room. There was no green car or dogcatcher. And Big Bill wasn't in his room. It was all a bad dream.

"You know what, Poppi?" said Maxi. "I think you're right."

"About what?" asked Poppi.

"I think rules do make us happier," said Maxi.

LET'S TALK ABOUT THIS

What this story teaches: We should obey God's rules and family rules for that will make us happy.

1. How do you feel about the rules in your family? Are you ever unhappy with them? What did you learn about rules from this story?
2. Why do you think God gave His rules, the Ten Commandments? How can they make us happy?

The Golden Calf
EXODUS 32

"If you please God, He will be with you and help you," Moses told his people.

The people were happy to hear this. "We will please Him," they said.

One day Moses returned to Mount Sinai. Joshua went part of the way with him. Then Moses went farther on, to talk with God. God gave Moses many new rules to share with his people.

Moses stayed in the mountain for many days, for God had much to tell him. As the days passed, the people began to wonder. At last some of them were sure that Moses was dead.

"Moses was wrong," they said. "God did not take care of Moses. So how can we expect God to take care of us?"

The people crowded around Aaron to talk with him about this. "Moses is gone," they said. "We want a god to lead us."

"Give me your gold," said Aaron.

The people brought their golden earrings to Aaron, and he melted them. From this he made a golden statue of a calf for the people to worship.

"Here is the god who brought us from Egypt," the people shouted.

Aaron was glad that the people had not started trouble. "Tomorrow we will have a big feast!" he said.

Early the next morning the people gave some offerings to their new god. Then they had a big feast, with eating and drinking, singing and dancing. The people were so excited that they began to do things that were evil—things God had told them not to do.

Back up in the mountains, God said to Moses, "You must go down to the camp now. The people have turned against Me. They are worshiping a golden calf they have made."

Moses left to get Joshua, and the two of them hurried down the mountain toward the camp. When they came near the camp, they could hear the shouting and singing of the people.

"Listen!" said Joshua. "Are they going to start a war?"

"No," Moses answered. "It is only the sound of singing."

The people were having so much fun that they had forgotten about Moses. But suddenly someone looked up at the mountain.

There was Moses, standing on a high ridge near the foot of the mountain. His face was filled with anger.

Soon others saw him, too. Before long the singing stopped, and all the camp became silent. The people trembled as they watched Moses come slowly into camp.

Moses knocked down the golden calf and ground it into powder. Then he spread the golden powder on some water.

"Drink it!" Moses commanded. One by one the people came and drank the water with the golden powder.

Then Moses turned to Aaron. "Why did you do this?" he demanded.

Aaron hung his head. "The people wanted a god," he said. "So we gathered their golden earrings and threw it into the fire. Suddenly, out came this calf."

The Lord was angry because the people had sinned so greatly against Him. That day many of the people died because of their sin. It was a sad day for the people of Israel. They had promised to obey the Lord and please Him. But they had turned against Him to worship another god.

God had promised them great happiness. But because they disobeyed God, the golden statue had brought them great misery.

WHAT DO YOU THINK?

What this story teaches: God expects us to trust in Him instead of things.

1. Why did the people turn away from God when Moses did not return to camp? What should they have done?
2. Did the golden calf bring the happiness the people thought it would? Why not?

King of the
Ice Cream Castle

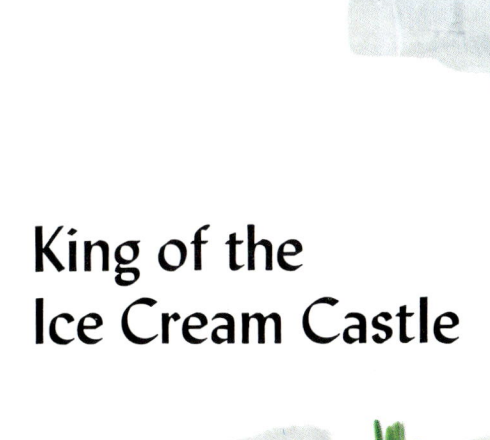

Maxi shook his bank but it didn't have the nice heavy feeling of a bank full of money. Instead, it sounded like a couple of lonely little coins were keeping each other company inside.

"I'm so hungry for a chocolate sundae," he moaned. "But it doesn't sound like there's enough to buy a spoonful."

Maxi turned the bank upside down and shook as hard as he could. One nickel fell out. Then another nickel fell and rolled across the table.

"I wonder how much of a chocolate sundae Pops would sell me for ten cents," Maxi complained.

He stuffed the two nickels into his pocket and walked out of the house. Ruff was sitting on the front steps.

"I suppose you always have enough money for your chocolate sundaes," Maxi grumbled.

Ruff cocked his head to one side and wagged his tail. He didn't know about this chocolate sundae thing, but he was glad to see Maxi come outside.

Tuff was sunning herself on the front lawn. "Dumb cat," Maxi grumbled. "You're too lazy to even go down to Pops for a chocolate sundae!"

Tuff lifted her head a little, blinked her eyes, then lay back down to sun herself. She was perfectly happy with a little cat food and some warm sunshine.

Maxi found an old stump and plopped himself on it to think. He had used the old stump one time for a wishing stump.

"Maybe I could wish for a chocolate sundae and it would happen," Maxi thought. "At least it would be fun to pretend."

Maxi had just started his wish when he heard someone calling his name.

"Maxi!"

"What are you doing here, Mini?"

"I came here to find you. What are you doing?"

"I'm just pretending."

"That's fun, Maxi. What are you pretending?"

"That I'm king of the ice cream castle. It's a great big castle and I'm the king. Each roof is made of chocolate. Whenever I want a chocolate sundae, I just go outside with a big dish and eat all I want."

"Sounds yummy, Maxi. But why are you frowning?"

"Well, it's that big flock of birds that just flew up."

"Birds? What birds?"

"The ones that are flying onto the roof of my castle. They're eating one of the chocolate roofs! Mini, what will I do?"

"Call out the guard, King Maxi," Mini shouted.

Before the twinkling of an eye, the peppermint soldiers came riding out on their marshmallow horses. They rode out to do battle with the birds. But some of the big birds flew down and captured the marshmallow horses in their beaks. Then they soared away to their nests high in the forest.

The battle was long and fierce. At last the peppermint soldiers won, but not before they had lost many of their brave marshmallow horses.

King Maxi was sad to see the losses in the great battle. In addition to the marshmallow horses they had lost a large part of a chocolate roof and some of the peppermint soldiers were chipped and broken.

But as King Maxi went across the moat into his ice cream castle he saw something moving. Then he noticed that it was an army of hungry children led by General Big Bill.

"We have come for chocolate sundaes!" shouted the general.

"But it would take the whole castle to feed you," King Maxi shouted back.

"Then we will capture the castle and eat it," General Big Bill shouted back.

King Maxi ordered the drawbridge pulled up just in time. But General Big Bill and some of his army of hungry children made rafts and got across the moat. Before long the ice cream castle was badly damaged.

At last King Maxi drove off the hungry army. Tired and disappointed, he lay down to sleep.

In the morning the sun rose. But instead of the friendly sun that had gone to bed the night before, it was a mischievous looking sun.

"Let's see what I can do to that ice cream castle," said the mischievous sun.

The sun shown so brightly that hot winds began to blow upon the castle. The castle began to melt.

"Stop! Stop!" shouted King Maxi.

But the mischievous sun would not stop. Slowly the great castle melted and King Maxi looked upon his kingdom. It was nothing but a puddle of melted chocolate and ice cream.

"It was a long hard fight," King Maxi said as he sat wearily on the stump.

"I know," said Mini. "You tried, but the birds and the hungry children and the mischievous sun were too much for you."

Maxi looked up from his pretend world. "I know what's wrong," he said. "I was just like the people who trusted the golden calf in the Bible story last night."

"How's that, Maxi?" Mini asked.

"Poppi said we can never depend on things because they melt away just when we need them," Maxi answered.

"But we can always depend on God," said Mini.

"Yeah, I guess that's right," said Maxi. "Let's go home."

"Aren't you coming with me to Pop's Sweet Shop?" asked Mini.

"With my two nickels?" said Maxi.

"No silly, with the dollar Poppi gave me for chocolate sundaes," said Mini. "He asked me to go find you."

"Well why didn't you say so," said Maxi. "We could have saved ourselves three battles and one melted castle!"

So Maxi and Mini laughed about that one all the way to Pop's Sweet Shop.

LET'S TALK ABOUT THIS

What this story teaches: We should trust in God instead of things, for God is always there to help us while things pass away.

1. How does rust, or rot, or melted ice cream remind you that things won't last? What did Maxi find from his pretend castle about trusting things?

2. Why did Maxi's pretend castle remind him of the golden calf in the Bible story? Can you think of some things that you trust in too much? Who should you trust completely? Will He ever let you down?

A House for God in the Wilderness

EXODUS 35—40

"We will build a house for God here in the wilderness," Moses told his people. "It will be a beautiful tent which we will carry with us as we travel."

The people were pleased to hear this. In Egypt their neighbors had worshiped their gods in beautiful temples. Why shouldn't their God have a beautiful house where they could worship Him?

"Bring your best gifts for God's house," Moses said. "We need gold, silver, wood, precious stones, beautiful cloth, and skins. But you must bring only what you want to give."

Moses asked those who could sew and work with metals and cloth to help, too. They would take the gifts and use them to make God's house.

Most of the people really wanted to give, and so they brought their best for God's house. Some came with gold and silver and precious stones. Others brought cloth and animal skins. And some brought wood or bronze.

Soon there was more than enough to build the beautiful tent. But still the people brought their gifts.

"Stop!" said Moses. "Do not bring any more gifts. We have more than enough now!"

The people were sorry to hear that. It was fun to share their best with God.

Many came to work on God's house. Moses put two men in charge of the work.

"These men have great skills in making things," Moses told the people. "They will use their skills for God's house. And you may use your skills, too."

Day after day the people worked on the great tent. Those who did not work often came to watch. The children came to watch, too.

"Look at those beautiful curtains," some said.

"See the golden cherubim on that chest," said others. "They look like angels."

One day the work was finished. It was time now to move the golden furniture into God's tent house, called the tabernacle. Moses was pleased to see how well the work had been done. The people were pleased, too.

When everything was in place, a cloud moved over the tent and covered the top. It was the large, special cloud in which God moved before His people.

"God has come to His new tabernacle," said the people.

The special cloud remained over the tabernacle through the day. When night came, the cloud began to glow, looking like beautiful firelight.

"God is staying at His tent house," the people said.

The people were pleased, for they had given their best for God, and God had accepted it. Now they knew that God was pleased with their gifts.

WHAT DO YOU THINK?

What this story teaches: God is pleased when we give good gifts for His house.

1. How did the people know that God had accepted their gifts? Why did this please them?
2. Why do you think God was pleased with His tent house? What if the people had not given their best? What kind of tabernacle would they have built then?

The Tabernacle Jar

"This is a special project," the Sunday school superintendent said. "We are going to see how much you kids can do toward decorating this room with new pictures and things."

Maxi and Mini were excited as they told Poppi and Mommi about the project. "And we're all going to help do it!" they said.

"That will be fun," said Mommi.

"And you will all appreciate it so much more because you do have a part," said Poppi.

"That reminds me of the story of the tabernacle which we just read," said Mommi. "All of the people brought their best gifts to help with God's house."

Maxi thought about the tabernacle that afternoon and how the people had given so many of their beautiful things for God's house. "But what could we give?" he asked Mini. "Most of our things wouldn't be what we need in our Sunday school room."

"Well, maybe it's not what we give, but what we give up," said Mini.

"Give up?" asked Maxi. "What do you mean?"

"The people gave their gold and wood and things to make God's house," said Mini. "But we don't have gold and skins and things for God's house."

"Yeah, and our superintendent doesn't need gold and skins," Maxi added. "He needs our dimes and nickels and quarters to help fix up our room."

141

"So why don't we give up something each day that we want to buy and put the money into a big jar," said Mini.

"That's it!" said Maxi. "A jar for God's house. We can call it the church jar. Or the jar for God's house."

"Or the tabernacle jar!" chimed Mini.

"Great!" Maxi agreed.

The next day Maxi began to think of a chocolate sundae. "Let's go down to Pop's Sweet Shop and get one for each of us," he suggested to Mini.

"Uh, uh!" said Mini. "Remember our tabernacle jar. That's something we can do without."

Maxi almost looked a little glum as he and Mini dropped some quarters and nickels into their tabernacle jar. But then he smiled as he thought of God's people giving to the real tabernacle.

This gave Maxi another idea. From an old Sunday school paper he cut a picture of the tabernacle and pasted it on one side of the tabernacle jar. On the other side he pasted a picture of their church which he had cut from a church bulletin.

On Tuesday Maxi almost bought a Gordon Hotfoot record, which was one of his favorites, but he remembered the tabernacle jar and put the money in it instead. Mini gave up a horn for her little bike on Thursday. And they each gave up souvenirs when they visited the museum with some friends. All those dimes and nickels and quarters went into the tabernacle jar.

On Sunday Maxi and Mini took their tabernacle jar to Sunday school and showed it to the superintendent.

"This is great," he said. "Let's show it to the rest of the department."

When he did several of the others decided they would make tabernacle jars, too. Then they would all bring their jars the last Sunday of that month and have a dedication service.

"We will each bring our jar up and give it to the Lord for His house," they said, "just like the people of Israel did for God's house in the wilderness."

So they did.

LET'S TALK ABOUT THIS

What this story teaches: We should give good gifts for God's house, for that will please Him and us.

1. How was the Sunday school project like the tabernacle project in the wilderness? Why do you think Maxi and Mini were happy to give up some things they wanted for this project?
2. What would you think if your church and Sunday school were taken away and you could never go there again? How would you feel about that? What would you give up for God's house? What else can you do to help make God's house a happy place?

Mini's Word List

Twelve words that all Minis and Maxis want to know.

ANGEL—A special kind of person who lives in heaven with God. Angels were sent to earth with special messages from God. They probably looked like people for Bible persons often thought they were looking at people when angels came to see them.

CARAVAN—People in Bible times usually did not travel alone because of robbers. Instead they walked together to another city or rode together on donkeys, on camels, or in carts.

FRANKINCENSE—A whitish-yellow resin that comes from a terebinth tree. It was valuable for it gave a pleasant smell.

INN—There were no hotels or motels in Bible times. Travelers stayed in homes or at inns. The inn was a building without furniture where people slept. Animals were kept in an open yard.

MIRACLE—God runs His world by certain rules or laws. People expect things to happen this same way all the time. But sometimes God does things in a special way. Jesus did many miracles, showing the people that He was God's Son.

MYRRH—Myrrh is a gum that drips from certain shrubs in the desert. Like frankincense, myrrh has a pleasant smell. Bible people thought it was very valuable.

PASSOVER—The night before God freed the people of Israel from their slavery in Egypt, He told them to sprinkle blood on their doorposts. When the angel of death came through Egypt, it passed over the houses with the blood. Since that time the Jewish people have celebrated this with a feast called Passover.

PROMISE—To promise is to say that you will do something that you intend to do.

SABBATH—One day each week used by the Jewish people of Bible times for rest. The Sabbath was patterned from the day when God rested from His creation.

TABERNACLE—The tabernacle was the large tent which the people of Israel used in the wilderness as a place of worship.

TEMPLE—The temple was a great building where the people of Israel came to worship God. The temple was in Jerusalem.

THE HOLY PLACE—The Holy Place was a special room inside the temple or tabernacle where only the priests could go at certain times to burn incense or worship.